creative *touches*

HOW TO ADD FLAIR TO READY-TO-WEAR

*Creating a fun, fashionable wardrobe has
never been easier than it is today. There's an abundance
of ready-made garments that are perfect for the latest craft
trend — wonderful wearable art. With our imaginative ideas
to guide you and a few basic notions and paints, you can
transform economical T-shirts, sweats, and other clothing
into creative fashions. In the process, you'll develop
your own personal style and gain a wealth of satisfaction!
This book is filled with easy-to-make,
fun-to-wear embellished clothing for the entire family. In
it, we show you how to take simple purchased pieces — many
of which you may already have in your closet — and create
your own designer wardrobe. You'll find shirts, pants, skirts,
and even dresses, and we've included lots of coordinating
accessories to help you achieve that polished, put-together look.
We know you'll enjoy making these
stylish projects. The creative touches they feature are sure to
help you build a wardrobe that's exclusively yours!*

Anne Childs

LEISURE ARTS, INC.
Little Rock, Arkansas

creative touches
HOW TO ADD FLAIR TO READY-TO-WEAR

EDITORIAL STAFF

Editor: Anne Van Wagner Childs
Executive Director: Sandra Graham Case
Creative Art Director: Gloria Bearden
Executive Editor: Susan Frantz Wiles

PRODUCTION

TECHNICAL
Managing Editor: Sherry Taylor O'Connor
Senior Technical Writer: Dawn R. Kelliher
Technical Writers: Nancy L. Taylor and
  Kathy R. Bradley

DESIGN
Design Director: Patricia Wallenfang Sowers
Designers: Diana Heien Suttle, Mary Lillian Hill, and
  Kimberly A. Hochstetler

EDITORIAL
Associate Editor: Dorothy Latimer Johnson
Senior Editorial Writer: Linda L. Trimble
Advertising and Direct Mail Copywriters:
  Laurie R. Burleson, Steven M. Cooper, and
  Eva M. Sargent

ART
Production Art Director: Melinda Stout
**Senior Production Artist/Advertising and Direct
  Mail Artist:** Linda Lovette
Art Production Assistants: Michael Spigner and
  Stephen L. Mooningham
Photography Stylists: Karen Smart Hall,
  Judith Howington Merritt, and Sondra Daniel
Typesetters: Cindy Lumpkin and Stephanie Cordero

BUSINESS STAFF

Publisher: Steve Patterson
Controller: Tom Siebenmorgen
Retail Sales Director: Richard Tignor
Retail Marketing Director: Pam Stebbins
Retail Customer Services Director: Margaret Sweetin
Marketing Manager: Russ Barnett

Executive Director of Marketing and Circulation:
  Guy A. Crossley
Fulfillment Manager: Scott Sharpe
Print Production: Nancy Reddick Lister and
  Laura Lockhart

MEMORIES IN THE MAKING SERIES

Hardcover ISBN 0-942237-16-1
Softcover ISBN 0-942237-86-2

TABLE OF CONTENTS

TABLE OF CONTENTS

Spring

When the warm sunny days of spring arrive, we look forward to getting outdoors for leisurely picnics and strolls. The change of season encourages us to step out in clothes that are light and cheerful, but a lingering chill in the air makes us reach for a sweatshirt or wrap now and then. Many of spring's casual get-togethers call for fun, comfortable clothing. Special occasions like Easter and Mother's Day, though, need dressy outfits trimmed with the finest lace and flowers.

To help you perk up your wardrobe for this wonderful season, we're pleased to present this collection of ideas that are as fresh and new as springtime itself.

Easter Bonnet, page 32

Adding springtime touches to ordinary accessories is fun — and easy! No one will believe that the precious chicks on our toddler's sailor hat were created with pom-poms. Bright jelly beans and polka-dotted ribbons are a quick way to jazz up a pair of plain canvas shoes.

"Chicky" Sailor Hat, page 24
Jelly Bean Shoes, page 26

*A*ny young miss will like this stylish cardigan! Perfect for the first cool days of spring, the colorful wrap is made from a sweatshirt, using a combination of simple sewing and painting.

Easter Egg
Shirt, page 32
Springtime
Cardigan, page 28

*Y*ou'll be stepping out in style when you wear this oversized T-shirt. The gaily colored eggs are easy to appliqué using our no-sew method.

9

Bunnies and chicks abound on these cute creations for little folks! Sweet little cross stitch designs make clothes for baby extra special. Boys will like the painted bunny shirt teamed with spatter-painted jeans and a cap. Floppy-eared bunnies adorn a jumper and shoes that are sure to delight a little girl.

Baby T-Shirts, page 35

Boys' Bunny Outfit,
page 29
Bunny Jumper
and Shoes, page 30

11

Y̶ou'll be captivatingly comfortable in this collection of rose-kissed nightwear. Embroidered blossoms give a cotton gown a sweet, delicate look, and bedroom slippers are adorned with doilies and ribbon roses. Men's short pajamas take on feminine appeal when dressed up with Battenburg lace and ribbon roses. Stenciled long-stemmed roses transform a terry robe into classy loungewear.

Embroidered Nightgown, page 26
Rosy Slippers and Battenburg Pajamas, page 33

Rose-Stenciled Robe, page 24

M*other and daughter will be picture-pretty in these matching dresses! Perfect for Easter or Mother's Day, the dresses are touched with the timeless beauty of Battenburg lace. For mother, a purchased T-shirt dress is adorned with romantic accents. The dainty daughter's dress begins with an ordinary T-shirt — the crisp skirt is made from a lace-trimmed table topper.*

Ladies' Battenburg Dress, page 23
Girls' Battenburg Dress, page 20

*C*lassic monograms and lace lend elegance to everyday clothes. To add the look of delicate French handsewing to a ready-made blouse without all the work, we used a simple lace insertion technique. A traditional monogram makes a shirt for Dad especially nice, and our floral monogram adorns a hair bow that coordinates with the blouse and other items in this collection.

Lace-Trimmed Blouse, page 22
Monogrammed Hair Bow and
Gentlemen's Monogram, page 26

Skirt with Handkerchief Pockets, page 24

With simple embellishments like these, it's easy — and inexpensive — to create a lovely wardrobe. A flowing skirt is given a sweet old-fashioned look by adding contrasting pockets featuring cuffs made from a vintage handkerchief. Appliquéd roses twine about a "trellis" on a pretty pink cardigan, and a feminine monogram dresses up a crisp white camp shirt. There's a matching hair bow on page 15.

Ladies' Monogram, page 26
Trellis Cardigan, page 31

On a warm spring afternoon, there's nothing nicer than relaxing outdoors among the flowers. For cute-as-a-button comfort, a shorts set made from men's pajamas is accented with a gathering of fabric flowers and other trims; slip-on canvas shoes are decorated to match. For cooler days, an appliquéd sweatshirt features a basket of beautiful blossoms.

Shoes, page 25
Flower Basket Sweatshirt, page 34

PJ's Shorts Set, page 25

Note: This project is suitable for girls' sizes 6 - 12.

You will need a white crew neck T-shirt, one 34" dia. white table topper with Battenburg lace trim (for skirt), two 16" square white napkins with Battenburg lace motif on 1 corner (for collar, dickey, and cuffs), Battenburg lace motifs (for waistline; we cut ours from table linens), white single-fold bias tape, white thread, one ½" dia. VELCRO® brand hook and loop fastener, 1⅛ yds of 1½"w white satin ribbon, string, thumbtack, safety pin, and removable fabric marking pen.

1. Wash, dry, and press shirt, napkins, table topper, and lace motifs.

2. For collar, dickey, and cuff pieces, place napkins right sides together. Referring to Diagram, page 21, use fabric marking pen and a ruler to mark cutting lines on wrong side of top napkin. Cutting through both napkins, cut out pieces. Mark wrong side of each piece.

3. Referring to Fig. 1, use fabric marking pen to draw a 10" line down center front of shirt. Beginning at shoulder seam, draw a straight line from each side of neckline to bottom of center line (Fig. 1).

Fig. 1

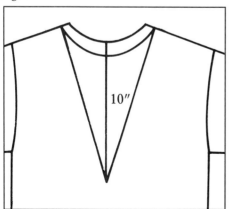

4. For collar, stitch ½" from raw edge of each collar piece. Matching right sides, refer to Fig. 2 to match stitched line on 1 collar piece to drawn line on shirt; pin in place. Beginning at bottom of collar piece and stitching to shoulder seam of shirt, stitch collar piece to shirt along stitched line on collar piece. Press collar piece to right side. Repeat to attach remaining collar piece to left side of shirt.

Fig. 2

5. To finish collar front, cut shirt open along marked center line; press excess shirt to wrong side along collar seams. Trim excess shirt ½" from collar seam; blindstitch in place.

6. To finish back neckline, measure along bottom of remaining shirt neckband from shoulder seam to shoulder seam; add 1". Cut bias tape the determined measurement. Unfold ends of tape and press ends ½" to wrong side. With right sides facing, pin 1 long raw edge of binding to back of shirt below neckband. Using a ¼" seam allowance, sew binding to shirt. Trim neckband from shirt. Press binding to wrong side of shirt; blindstitch in place.

7. Referring to Fig. 3, trim top point of 1 collar piece ½" from shirt shoulder seam. Press raw edge ½" to wrong side; blindstitch folded edge in place along shoulder seam. Repeat for remaining collar piece.

Fig. 3

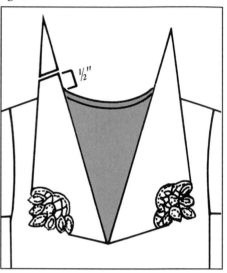

8. Referring to Fig. 4, place dickey pieces right sides up with top edge of top dickey piece ¾" below top edge of bottom dickey piece; pin in place. Trim raw edges of top piece even with raw edges of bottom piece.

Fig. 4

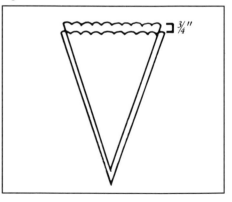

9. To finish raw edges of dickey, use a medium zigzag stitch with a medium stitch length to stitch ¼" from raw edges. Trim edges close to stitching.

10. Place dickey inside neckline; adjust to fit. Pin in place. On wrong side of shirt, hand stitch dickey to shirt along 1 side of collar, being careful not to catch collar in stitching. Hand stitch dickey halfway up remaining side of collar. Following manufacturer's instructions, stitch hook and loop fastener to open side of neckline and to dickey.

11. For sleeve cuffs, measure circumference of sleeve opening; add 1". If necessary, trim length of cuff pieces to the determined measurement.

12. Cut off sleeve ¼" above hem stitching line. Matching right sides and short edges, fold 1 cuff piece in half. Use a ½" seam allowance to sew short edges together; press seam open. With right side of cuff facing wrong side of sleeve and matching seams and raw edges, insert cuff into sleeve; pin in place. Use a ½" seam allowance to sew cuff to sleeve. Fold cuff to right side; press. Repeat for remaining cuff.

13. For skirt, fold table topper in half from top to bottom and again from left to right. To determine skirt opening size, measure the width of the bottom front of the shirt; divide by 3. Tie 1 end of string to fabric marking pen. Insert thumbtack through string the determined measurement from pen. Referring to Fig. 5, insert thumbtack in fabric and mark ¼ of a circle. Cutting through all thicknesses, cut out skirt along marked line. Remove all pen marks.

Fig. 5

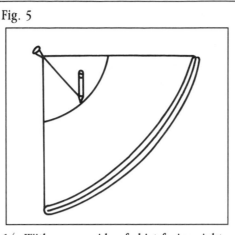

14. With wrong side of skirt facing right side of shirt, overlap raw edge of skirt 1½" over bottom edge of shirt; easing shirt as necessary, pin in place. Check placement of skirt by trying garment on child; adjust as necessary. Baste in place.

15. Using a medium zigzag stitch with a medium stitch length, stitch skirt to shirt along raw edge; press.

16. To cover raw edge of skirt, arrange lace motifs over raw edge, overlapping motifs if necessary; pin in place. Hand stitch motifs in place.

17. Remove all visible basting threads and pen marks; press.

18. Tie ribbon into a bow; trim ends. Use safety pin on wrong side of dress to pin bow to bottom center of collar.

19. To launder, remove bow and hand wash in warm water; hang to dry.

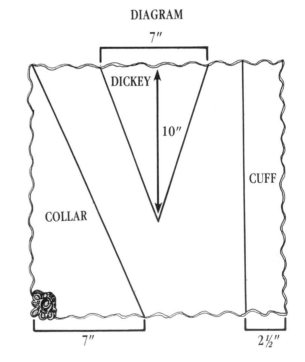

DIAGRAM

7"

DICKEY

10"

CUFF

COLLAR

7"

2½"

LACE-TRIMMED BLOUSE (Shown on page 15)

You will need a blouse (we used a short-sleeved, jewel-neck shell with bias binding at neckline), ½″w insertion lace (lace with 2 straight edges), 1″w lace edging (lace with 1 scalloped edge and 1 straight edge), removable fabric marking pen, seam ripper, and thread to match lace.

1. Wash, dry, and press blouse and laces. Use seam ripper to remove neck binding from blouse; set aside.
2. Referring to blue lines on Blouse Front Diagram for placement of insertion lace on blouse front, follow Steps 1 - 8 of Applying Insertion Lace instructions.
3. Referring to grey lines on Blouse Front Diagram for placement of lace edging on blouse front, follow Steps 1 - 4 of Applying Insertion Lace instructions.
4. To finish neck edge, trim ends of lace even with top of blouse. Replace neck binding.
5. To finish blouse hem, press ends of lace to wrong side of blouse and whipstitch in place.
6. Referring to blue line on Sleeve Diagram for placement of insertion lace on each sleeve, follow Steps 1 - 6 of Applying Insertion Lace instructions.
7. Referring to grey line on Sleeve Diagram for placement of lace edging on each sleeve, follow Steps 1 - 4 of Applying Insertion Lace instructions.
8. Turn blouse wrong side out. Press each sleeve hem to wrong side along lace edging stitching line. Follow Steps 7 - 9 of Applying Insertion Lace instructions.

APPLYING INSERTION LACE
1. On right side of garment, use removable fabric marking pen to draw lines for placement of lace.

2. Measure length of each marked line; add 2″. For each marked line, cut 1 piece of lace the determined measurement.
3. Center lace pieces over marked lines; hand baste edges in place.
4. (*Note:* Use a narrow zigzag stitch with a short stitch length for Steps 4 - 9.) Stitch straight edges of each lace piece to garment. Remove all basting threads.
5. Turn garment wrong side out. Being careful not to cut lace, cut fabric along center between stitching lines (Fig. 1).

Fig. 1

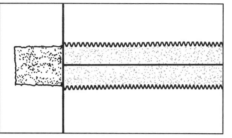

6. Press cut edges away from lace along stitching lines (Fig. 2).

Fig. 2

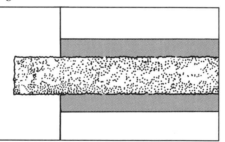

7. Turn garment right side out. Sewing through all layers of fabric, stitch along straight edges of lace pieces again.
8. Turn garment wrong side out. Trim excess fabric close to stitching lines. Turn right side out; press.
9. To secure lace ends at seamlines on sleeves, overlap lace ends. Referring to Fig. 3, stitch across lace. Trim excess lace close to stitching.

Fig. 3

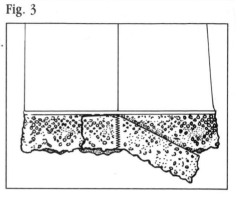

BLOUSE FRONT DIAGRAM

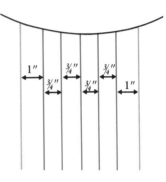

SLEEVE DIAGRAM

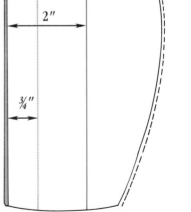

You will need a white T-shirt dress (we used a crew neck T-shirt dress with dropped waist and gathered skirt), two 12″ x 18″ white place mats with Battenburg lace trim (for collar), 1½″w white lace edging (lace with 1 scalloped edge and 1 straight edge; see Steps 3 and 6 for amount), ½″w insertion lace (lace with 2 straight edges; see Steps 3 and 6 for amount), 1⅓ yds of 2¼″w white satin ribbon and 2⅔ yds of ⅜″w lace edging (for bow), removable fabric marking pen, fabric glue, safety pin, and white thread.

1. Wash, dry, and press dress, place mats, and laces.
2. Drawing a 10½″ line down center front of dress, follow Step 3 of Girls' Battenburg Dress, page 20.
3. For yoke, refer to photo and blue lines on Diagram for insertion lace and grey lines on Diagram for lace edging and follow Steps 1 - 4 of Applying Insertion Lace (Lace-Trimmed Blouse, page 22).
4. To finish neck edge, use a narrow zigzag stitch with a short stitch length to stitch on dress close to neck binding seamline. Trim lace ends close to stitching.
5. For left side of collar, fold 1 place mat in half diagonally with wrong sides together; press. Unfold place mat. With right sides facing, refer to Fig. 1 and position place mat on dress front with corner of place mat at bottom point of yoke (place mat will extend past shoulder seam); pin in place. Beginning at bottom point of yoke and ending at shoulder seam, stitch place mat to dress along pressed line. Refold place mat along pressed line. Fold portion of collar extending beyond shoulder seam to back of dress; tack in place. Using

remaining place mat, repeat for remaining side of collar.

Fig. 1

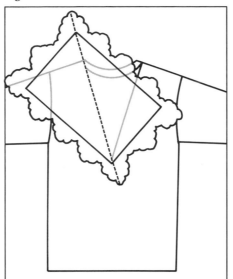

6. To determine lace pieces needed for waistline, sleeves, and hemline, measure circumference of each; add 2″ to each measurement. Cut the following lace pieces:

  Waistline - one 1½″ wide piece
  Sleeves - two 1½″ wide and two
    ½″ wide pieces
  Hemline - one 1½″ wide and one
    ½″ wide piece

7. For waistline, place scalloped edge of lace along waistline seam, overlapping ends at side seam; pin in place.
8. For lace at hem of sleeves and hem of dress, place scalloped edge of lace along bottom of hem, overlapping ends at side seam; pin in place.
9. For ½″ wide lace on sleeve, place bottom edge of lace ½″ above straight edge of 1½″ wide lace, overlapping ends at seam; pin in place. For ½″ wide lace on dress hem, place bottom edge of lace 1¼″ above straight edge of 1½″ wide lace,

overlapping ends at side seam; pin in place.
10. Hand baste lace pieces in place along all straight edges. Using a narrow zigzag stitch with a short stitch length, stitch over all basted edges of lace. Do not trim overlapped lace ends.
11. Turn dress wrong side out. For sleeve and dress hems, trim fabric underneath 1½″ wide lace close to stitching, being careful not to cut lace.
12. Turn dress right side out. Follow Step 9 of Applying Insertion Lace instructions (Lace-Trimmed Blouse, page 22) to secure and trim overlapping ends of lace.
13. Remove all visible basting threads and pen marks.
14. Glue ⅜″ wide lace edging to wrong side along both edges of ribbon. Allow to dry. Tie ribbon into a bow. Cut V-shaped notches in ends of ribbon. Use safety pin on wrong side of dress to pin bow to bottom center of collar.
15. To launder, remove bow and hand wash. Hang to dry.

DIAGRAM

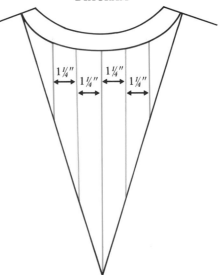

1¼″ 1¼″ 1¼″ 1¼″

ROSE-STENCILED ROBE

(Shown on page 13)

You will need a robe (we used a wrap-style terry velour robe), fabric paint, small stencil brushes, acetate for stencils (available at craft or art supply stores), craft knife, cutting mat or a thick layer of newspapers, paper towels, permanent felt-tip pen with fine point, removable tape (optional), and T-shirt form or cardboard covered with waxed paper.

Referring to photo, use rose pattern and follow Stenciling, page 126, to stencil designs on robe.

"CHICKY" SAILOR HAT

(Shown on page 8)

You will need a child's sailor hat, one 1⅝" dia. button, 22" of ⅞"w satin ribbon, six 20" lengths of ¹⁄₁₆"w satin ribbon, 3" of ½"w grosgrain ribbon, six ¾" dia. yellow pom-poms, six ⅜" dia. yellow pom-poms, black and red permanent felt-tip pens with fine points, black acrylic paint, small round paintbrush, and craft glue.

1. For top of hat, tie ⅞" wide ribbon into a double-loop bow. Cut V-shaped notches in ends of ribbon. Tie lengths of ¹⁄₁₆" wide ribbon together into a bow. Glue small bow to large bow; glue large bow to center of button. Thread ends of ½" wide ribbon through button holes from front to back. Glue ends of ribbon to back of button. Glue button to top of hat; allow to dry.

2. For chicks, refer to photo and glue pom-poms to brim of hat; allow to dry. Use red pen to draw beaks and black pen to draw legs and feet.

3. For eyes, paint black dots on ⅜" dia. pom-poms. Allow to dry.

SKIRT WITH HANDKERCHIEF POCKETS   (Shown on page 16)

You will need a gathered skirt without pockets, one approx. 15" square handkerchief, two 10" x 15" pieces of fabric for pockets, two 10" x 15" pieces of white fabric for pocket linings, lightweight fusible interfacing, tracing paper, removable fabric marking pen, transparent tape, and thread to match fabrics.

1. Wash, dry, and press skirt, fabrics, and handkerchief.

2. Use cuff pattern (shown in pink on page 25) and follow Tracing Patterns, page 124. Cut out pattern. Referring to Fig. 1 for pattern placement, use pattern and cut 2 cuff pieces from handkerchief. Press long raw edge of each cuff piece ¼" to wrong side.

Fig. 1

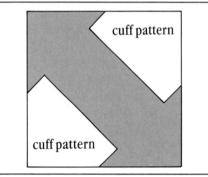

3. For pockets, use pocket pattern pieces (shown in grey on page 25) and follow Tracing Patterns, page 124. Cut out pattern pieces. Matching registration marks (⊕), overlap pattern pieces to form complete pattern; tape pattern pieces together.

4. (*Note:* Repeat Steps 4 - 6 for each pocket.) Following manufacturer's instructions, fuse interfacing to wrong side of 1 pocket fabric piece. Using pocket piece and 1 lining piece, use pocket pattern and follow Sewing Shapes, page 124, to make 1 pocket. Sew final closure by hand; press.

5. Referring to Fig. 2, place 1 cuff piece right side up on pocket lining, matching point of cuff piece to point of pocket lining. Sewing close to pressed edge of cuff piece, stitch cuff piece to pocket (Fig. 2).

Fig. 2

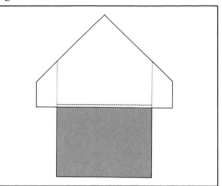

6. Press raw edges of cuff piece to right side of pocket. Referring to pocket pattern, press cuff to right side of pocket along dotted line.

7. Pin pockets to skirt. Check placement of pockets by trying skirt on; adjust if necessary.

8. Unfold cuff of 1 pocket. Beginning and ending at pressed line and stitching close to edges of pocket, sew side and bottom edges of pocket to skirt (Fig. 3). Repeat for remaining pocket.

Fig. 3

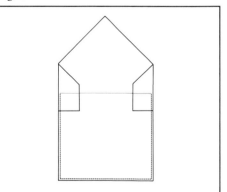

9. Refold cuffs. Blindstitch side edges of cuffs to edges of pockets; press.

PJ'S SHORTS SET AND SHOES (Shown on pages 18 and 19)

For shorts set, you will need men's short-sleeved short pajamas; six 5″ fabric squares for flowers; fabric for sleeve, pocket, and shorts trim (see Steps 2, 6, and 12 for amounts); 3 yds of ⅛″w satin ribbon; and ⅜″w lace trim (see Steps 2, 5, 6, and 12 for amounts).

For shoes, you will need slip-on canvas shoes, two 3¾″ dia. purchased crocheted doilies, eight 5″ fabric squares for flowers, and 1½ yds of ⅛″w satin ribbon.

You will also need washable fabric glue, thread to match fabrics, buttons, tracing paper, and compass.

SHORTS SET

1. Wash, dry, and press lace, fabrics, ribbon, and pajamas.

2. (*Note:* Follow Steps 2 - 4 for each sleeve.) For trim on sleeve, measure circumference of sleeve opening; add 1″. Cut a strip from fabric 4″ wide by the determined measurement. Cut a length of lace the determined measurement.

3. With straight edge (top) of lace ¼″ from 1 long edge (top) of fabric strip, baste lace to right side of fabric strip. Matching right sides and short edges, fold fabric strip in half. Use a ½″ seam allowance and sew short edges together to form a loop; press seam open.

Matching wrong sides and raw edges, fold in half; press.

4. With lace facing wrong side of sleeve, insert fabric trim in sleeve with pressed edge of trim extending 1⅝″ beyond edge of sleeve. Stitching close to edge of sleeve, sew trim to sleeve, being careful to catch straight edge of lace in stitching.

5. For lace trim at neckline, measure edge of front opening; add 1″. Cut a piece of lace the determined measurement. Press ends of lace ½″ to wrong side. Glue straight edge of lace to right side of front opening or placket.

6. For pocket trim, measure width of pocket; add 1″. Cut a strip from fabric 2¼″ wide by the determined measurement. Cut a length of lace the determined measurement.

7. Press raw edges of fabric strip ½″ to wrong side. Press ends of lace ½″ to wrong side. With ¼″ of lace extending beyond edge of strip, glue straight edge of lace to wrong side of strip along 1 long edge.

8. Referring to photo and matching edges of strip to top of pocket, glue strip to pocket. Allow to dry.

9. For flower patterns, use compass to draw one 3½″ dia. and one 4″ dia. circle on tracing paper; cut out. Use patterns and cut 1 large and 5 small circles from fabric squares.

10. For flowers, use a double strand of thread to baste ⅛″ from edge of 1 fabric circle. Pull ends of thread to tightly gather circle; knot thread and trim ends. Fold raw edges to inside of circle. With circle flattened and gathers at center, sew 1 button over opening. Repeat for remaining circles.

11. Cut six 18″ lengths from ribbon. Tie each length into a bow. Glue knot of 1 bow to back of each flower. Allow to dry. Refer to photo to arrange flowers on and above pocket; glue to secure. Arrange bow streamers and glue in place. Allow to dry.

12. For trim on shorts, repeat Steps 2 - 4 for each leg.

13. To launder, follow glue manufacturer's recommendations.

SHOES

1. Referring to photo, glue 1 doily to toe of each shoe.

2. For flowers, use compass to draw one 3″ dia. and one 3½″ dia. circle and repeat Steps 9 and 10 of Shorts Set instructions to make 2 large and 6 small flowers.

3. Cut ribbon into 8 equal lengths. Referring to photo, follow Step 11 of Shorts Set instructions, trimming streamers as desired.

fold line

POCKET

POCKET

25

EMBROIDERED NIGHTGOWN (Shown on page 12)

You will need a nightgown (we used a sleeveless cotton knee-length nightgown), tracing paper, hot-iron transfer pencil or other item(s) to transfer pattern to garment (see Transferring Patterns, page 124), pink and green embroidery floss (we used DMC 605 and DMC 955), and embroidery hoop.

1. Follow Tracing Patterns and Transferring Patterns, page 124, to transfer pattern to nightgown.
2. Using 2 strands of pink floss for roses and 2 strands of green floss for leaves, use Stem Stitch, page 127, to work design.

JELLY BEAN SHOES

(Shown on page 8)

You will need a pair of white canvas lace-up tennis shoes; tracing paper; purple, pink, green, yellow, orange, and white fabric paint; two 1 yd lengths of ⅞"w ribbon; and small paintbrushes.

1. Trace jelly bean pattern onto tracing paper; cut out.
2. (*Note:* Refer to photo for Steps 2 - 5.) Use a pencil to lightly draw around pattern on shoes.
3. Paint jelly beans; allow to dry.
4. Paint white highlight on each jelly bean; allow to dry.
5. Remove laces from shoes; relace shoes with ribbon lengths. Cut V-shaped notches in ends of ribbon.

MONOGRAMMED HAIR BOW

(Shown on page 15)

You will need a 5" square of white Jobelan (32 ct), 1 yd of 1½"w white satin ribbon, 1¼ yds of ⅝"w white satin ribbon, three 18" lengths of ¹⁄₁₆"w pink satin ribbon, 1⅞" dia. covered button kit, embroidery floss (see color key, page 27), 3" long hair clasp, white cloth-covered florist wire, hot glue gun, and glue sticks.

1. Centering design on fabric, work ladies' monogram, page 27, over 2 fabric threads using 2 strands of floss for Cross Stitch and 1 for Backstitch.
2. Centering stitched design on button, follow manufacturer's instructions to cover button with stitched piece.
3. Form ⅝"w ribbon into a triple-loop bow; wrap wire around center of bow to secure. Form 1½"w ribbon into a double-loop bow; wrap wire around center of bow to secure. Tie ¹⁄₁₆" w ribbon lengths together into a bow. Wire bows together.
4. Glue bows to hair clasp. Glue button over centers of bows.

LADIES' AND GENTLEMEN'S MONOGRAMS

(Shown on pages 15 and 17)

For ladies' monogram, you will need a shirt and a 3" square of 12 mesh waste canvas.
For men's monogram, you will need a men's oxford cloth shirt and a 1½" square of 18 mesh waste canvas.
You will also need embroidery hoop (optional), spray bottle filled with water, masking tape, lightweight non-fusible interfacing, thread, tweezers, and embroidery floss (see color key, page 27).

Referring to photo for placement, follow Working On Waste Canvas, page 127, to work design on shirt. For ladies' monogram, page 27, use 2 strands for Cross Stitch and 1 for Backstitch; for men's monogram, page 27, use 3 strands for Cross Stitch.

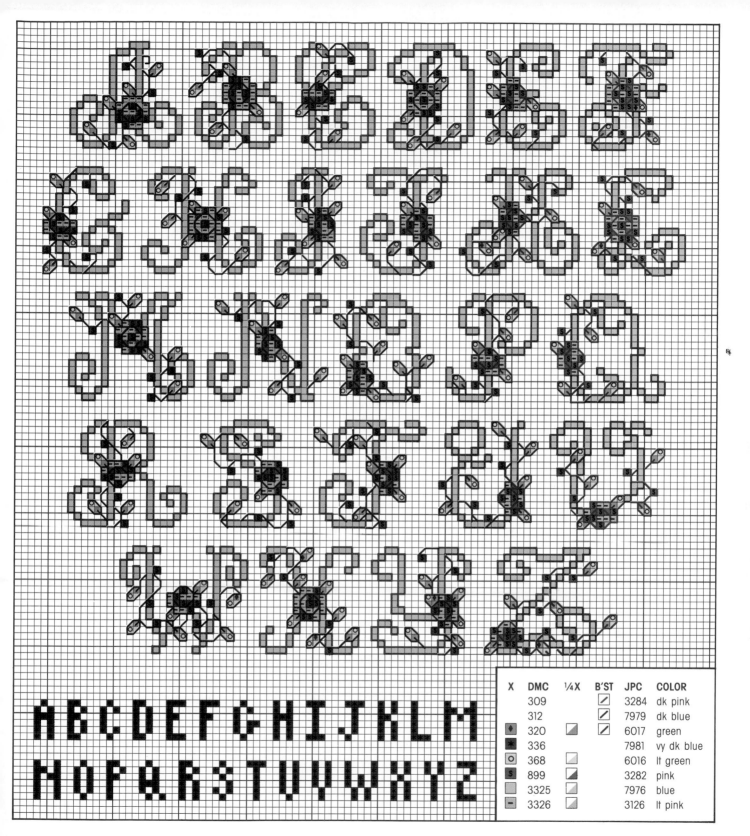

X	DMC	¼X	B'ST	JPC	COLOR
	309		╱	3284	dk pink
	312		╱	7979	dk blue
◆	320	◩	╱	6017	green
✳	336			7981	vy dk blue
○	368	◩		6016	lt green
S	899	◩		3282	pink
	3325	◩		7976	blue
−	3326	◩		3126	lt pink

You will need a sweatshirt, fabric for eggs, fabric for binding, 1"w bias tape to match sweatshirt, thread to match fabrics, lightweight fusible interfacing, paper-backed fusible web, ⅛"w and ¹⁄₁₆"w satin ribbon, ⅝"w rickrack, 1½"w pregathered eyelet trim, ½"w elastic, buttons, ⅜" dia. white pom-poms for tails, clear dimensional fabric paint in squeeze bottle, fabric paint, acetate for stencil (available at craft or art supply stores), T-shirt form or cardboard covered with waxed paper, removable fabric marking pen, tracing paper, black permanent felt-tip pen with fine point, paper towels, cutting mat or a thick layer of newspapers, craft knife, stencil brush, removable tape (optional), washable fabric glue, and see-through pressing cloth.

1. (*Note:* Refer to photo for Steps 1 - 3.) Use bunny pattern and fabric paint and follow Stenciling, page 126, to stencil bunnies on shirt, reversing stencil if desired.

2. For bunny eyes, use felt-tip pen to draw black dots on bunnies.

3. For eggs, use small egg pattern, page 32, and follow Tracing Patterns, page 124. Cut out pattern. Follow Steps 2 - 5 of Making Appliqués, page 124. To apply dimensional paint to edges of appliqués, follow Steps 2 - 6 of Dimensional Fabric Painting, page 125.

4. For front opening, use fabric marking pen to draw a line down center front of shirt from neckband to waistband. Cut shirt along marked line. Cut off waistband and sleeve ribbing.

5. To finish neckband, fold each cut edge of neckband diagonally to inside of shirt, matching cut edge to lower edge of neckband (Fig. 1); whipstitch edges in place.

Fig. 1

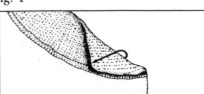

6. For rickrack trim, measure front opening from neckband to bottom edge of shirt. Cut 2 lengths of rickrack the determined measurement. Referring to photo, glue rickrack ¾" from each edge of front opening. Allow to dry.

7. For front opening binding, measure front opening from bottom of neckband to bottom of shirt, around bottom of shirt, and up left opening to bottom of neckband; add 1". For sleeve bindings, measure 1 sleeve opening; add 2". For neckband binding, measure around bottom of neckband; add 1". Cut bias strips 2" wide by the determined measurements. For ruffle, cut a length of eyelet trim the determined neck measurement.

8. Press ends of each bias strip ½" to wrong sides. Matching wrong sides, press each strip in half lengthwise. Press each long edge to center.

9. For neckband trim, press ends of eyelet trim ½" to wrong side. Insert straight edge of eyelet trim between long folded edges of neckband binding; baste in place. Referring to photo, position neckband trim below neckband of shirt; stitch in place close to each long edge of binding.

10. To bind raw edges of cardigan, begin with pressed end of bias strip at top of neckband trim. Insert raw edges of cardigan and neckband trim between long folded edges of binding; baste in place. Stitch all layers together close to inner edge of binding. Remove basting threads.

11. For sleeves, insert raw edge of sleeve between long folded edges of bias strip, overlapping ends of strip; baste in place. Sew all layers together close to inner edge of binding. Repeat for remaining sleeve.

12. Turn cardigan wrong side out. For sleeve casings, measure around 1 sleeve 2" from bottom edge. Cut bias tape 1" longer than the determined measurement. Press ends of bias tape ½" to wrong side. Matching wrong sides, pin bias tape to sleeve with 1 long edge of bias tape 2" from bottom edge of sleeve. Stitching close to each long edge of bias tape, sew tape in place. Measure wrist; add 1". Cut elastic the determined measurement. Thread elastic through casing. Overlap ends of elastic 1" and sew ends together. Whipstitch opening of casing closed. Repeat for remaining sleeve. Turn right side out.

13. Cut desired length of each width ribbon. Tie lengths together into a bow. Repeat to make desired number of bows.

14. Referring to photo, glue buttons and bows to cardigan. For bunny tails, glue pom-poms to bunnies; allow to dry.

15. For shirt closure, cut a 1" x 3" bias strip from fabric. With wrong sides together, press strip in half lengthwise; press long raw edges to center. Referring to Fig. 2, form a loop and tack to wrong side of right front opening. Referring to photo for placement, sew a button to left front opening.

Fig. 2

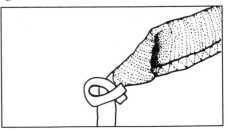

BOYS' BUNNY OUTFIT (Shown on page 11)

You will need a T-shirt, hat, pants, fabric paint (see color key for colors), tracing paper, item(s) to transfer pattern to shirt (see Transferring Patterns, page 124), one ¼″ dia. gold nail head, liner paintbrush, small round paintbrushes, toothbrush, and T-shirt form or cardboard covered with waxed paper.

1. Wash, dry, and press shirt and pants according to paint manufacturer's recommendations.

2. (*Note:* Refer to photo for Steps 2 - 5.) Use bunny pattern and follow Tracing Patterns and Transferring Patterns, page 124, to transfer pattern to shirt.

3. Insert T-shirt form into shirt. Referring to photo and color key and allowing paint to dry between colors, paint design.

4. Follow manufacturer's instructions to attach nail head to top of bunny hat.

5. For pants and hat, use green, yellow, blue, and pink paint and follow Spatter Painting, page 126.

6. Follow paint manufacturer's instructions to heat-set paint if necessary.

7. To launder, follow paint manufacturer's recommendations.

COLOR KEY
Fur - beige
Nose and inner ear - pink
Eyes - white, blue, and black
Teeth - white
Hat - yellow and green
Outline, whiskers, and freckles - black

BUNNY JUMPER AND SHOES (Shown on page 11)

For jumper, you will need a garment with pocket large enough to accommodate design (we used a denim jumper), four 3″ x 7″ pieces of white fabric for ears, 21″ of ⅞″w satin ribbon, and a safety pin.

For shoes, you will need a pair of white lace-up canvas tennis shoes with toe area large enough to accommodate design, eight 3″ x 5″ pieces of white fabric for ears, 30″ of ⅜″w satin ribbon, two 1½″ dia. white pom-poms, washable fabric glue, and a seam ripper.

You will also need tracing paper, item(s) to transfer patterns to garments (see Transferring Patterns, page 124), paper towels, black permanent felt-tip pen with fine point, paintbrushes, white thread, medium weight fusible interfacing, and fabric paint (see color key for colors).

JUMPER

1. Wash, dry, and press garment and fabric according to paint manufacturer's recommendations.

2. (*Note:* Refer to photo for Steps 2 - 9.) Follow Tracing Patterns and Transferring Patterns, page 124, to transfer large bunny face to pocket.

3. Referring to color key and allowing to dry between colors, paint and outline design.

4. Use a dry paintbrush and dip tips of bristles in pink paint. Brush tips across paper towels to remove excess paint. Lightly stroke brush across center of each cheek; allow to dry.

5. Follow paint manufacturer's instructions to heat-set paint if necessary.

6. Follow Tracing Patterns, page 124, to trace large ear pattern, page 31. Cut out pattern.

7. For ears, follow manufacturer's instructions to fuse interfacing to wrong side of 1 fabric piece. Using interfaced fabric piece and another fabric piece, follow Sewing Shapes, page 124, to make 1 ear. Sew final closure by hand; press. Repeat for remaining ear.

8. Repeat Steps 4 and 5 to paint center of each ear.

9. Securely tack ears to inside of pocket.

10. Tie ribbon into a bow; trim ends. Use safety pin on inside of pocket to pin bow between ears.

11. To launder, remove bow and follow paint manufacturer's recommendations.

SHOES

1. For left shoe, follow Tracing Patterns and Transferring Patterns, page 124, to transfer small bunny face pattern to shoe. Turn pattern over and repeat for right shoe.

2. Omitting white paint, follow Steps 3 and 4 of Jumper instructions to paint design.

3. Use small ear pattern, page 31, and follow Steps 6 - 8 of Jumper instructions to make 4 ears.

4. Cutting through all layers, use seam ripper to make a slit in each ear where indicated by dotted line on pattern. Unlace shoes and thread 2 ears onto center of each shoe lace. Refer to Fig. 1, page 31, to relace shoes.

SMALL BUNNY

COLOR KEY
Cheeks - white
Eyes - white, blue, and black
Nose - pink
Mouth - dk pink and black
Outline and eyelashes - black permanent
   pen

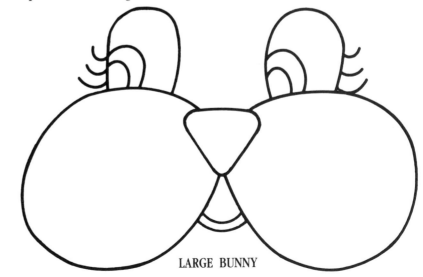

LARGE BUNNY

BUNNY JUMPER AND SHOES
(continued)

Fig. 1

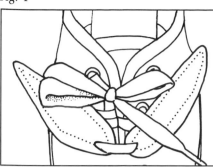

5. Cut ribbon in half. For each shoe, tie 1 length of ribbon into a bow around bottom bar formed by shoe laces.

6. For tails, glue 1 pom-pom to heel of each shoe.

LARGE
EAR
(make 2)

SMALL EAR
(make 4)

TRELLIS CARDIGAN   (Shown on page 17)

You will need a cardigan (we used a cotton jersey knit cardigan), floral print fabric, permanent felt-tip pen with fine point and permanent felt-tip pen with wide point to coordinate with fabric, lightweight fusible interfacing, paper-backed fusible web, clear glitter dimensional fabric paint in squeeze bottle, buttons to coordinate with cardigan, thread to match buttons, yardstick, removable fabric marking pen, and T-shirt form or cardboard covered with waxed paper.

1. Wash, dry, and press cardigan and fabric according to paint manufacturer's recommendations. Insert T-shirt form in cardigan.

2. Referring to Diagram, use yardstick and fabric marking pen to lightly draw lines on cardigan.

3. Referring to photo, use permanent pen with fine point to draw over pen lines.

4. Use permanent pen with fine point to draw lines $\frac{1}{4}''$ to the right and left of the vertical lines. Repeat to draw lines $\frac{1}{4}''$ above and below horizontal lines.

5. Referring to photo, use permanent pen with wide point to draw over center lines.

6. Follow manufacturer's instructions to fuse interfacing then web to wrong side of fabric.

7. Cut floral motifs from fabric; remove paper backing. Refer to photo to arrange cutouts on cardigan. Fuse cutouts to cardigan.

8. Replace buttons.

9. Use paint and follow Steps 2 - 7 of Dimensional Fabric Painting, page 125, to paint over raw edges of cutouts.

DIAGRAM

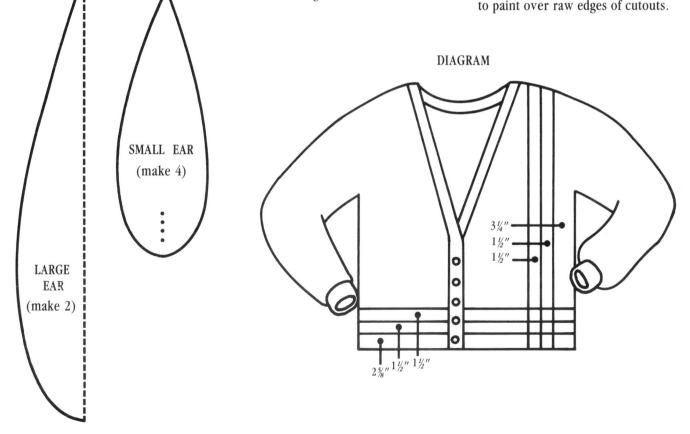

31

EASTER EGG SHIRT

(Shown on page 9)

You will need a T-shirt, fabrics for appliqués, buttons, ribbon, lace trim, rickrack, lightweight fusible interfacing, paper-backed fusible web, see-through pressing cloth, T-shirt form or cardboard covered with waxed paper, washable fabric glue, clear dimensional fabric paint in squeeze bottle, and tracing paper.

1. Use small, medium, and large egg patterns and follow Tracing Patterns, page 124. Cut out patterns.
2. (*Note*: Refer to photo for Steps 2 - 7.) For egg appliqués, use patterns and follow Making Appliqués, page 124.
3. Measure circumference of shirt 1″ below neck opening; add 1″. Cut rickrack the determined measurement. Overlapping ends at center back, glue rickrack to shirt 1″ below neck opening. Allow to dry.
4. Measure circumference of 1 sleeve; add 1″. Cut 2 pieces of rickrack the determined measurement. Overlapping ends at sleeve seam and placing rickrack 1″ and 2″ from edge of sleeve, glue rickrack to sleeve. Allow to dry. Repeat for remaining sleeve.
5. Glue lace, ribbon, and rickrack to large and medium eggs; trim ends even with edges of eggs. Allow to dry.
6. Glue buttons to shirt; allow to dry.
7. Follow Steps 2 - 7 of Dimensional Fabric Painting, page 125, to apply paint to edges of eggs.

EASTER BONNET   (Shown on page 7)

You will need a straw hat, fabric for hatband and bow (see Steps 1 and 5 for amount), 30″ of 1″w satin ribbon, four 26″ lengths of desired width satin ribbon, ½″w lace trim (see Step 1 for amount), thread to match fabric, silk flowers, gesso, white and desired colors of acrylic paint, removable fabric marking pen, paintbrushes, paper towels, fabric glue, hot glue gun, and glue sticks.

1. For hatband, measure circumference of hat crown; add 2″. Cut a strip of fabric 2½″ wide by the determined measurement. Cut 2 lengths of lace the determined measurement.
2. Matching right sides, fold fabric strip in half lengthwise. Use a ¼″ seam allowance to sew long edges together. Turn right side out. With seam at center back, press strip.
3. Use fabric glue to glue lace trim along both edges of hatband. Allow to dry.
4. Refer to photo to hot glue hatband around hat.
5. For fabric bow, cut a 4½″ x 36″ strip from fabric. Matching right sides, press strip in half lengthwise. Referring to Fig. 1, use fabric marking pen to mark stitching line at each end of bow strip. Leaving an opening for turning, sew strip together along stitching line at each end and ¼″ from long raw edge. Cut corners diagonally and turn right side out; press. Sew final closure by hand. Tie into a bow.

Fig. 1

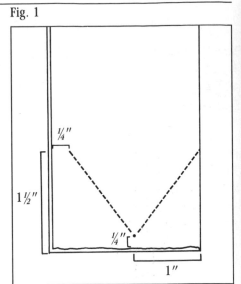

6. Hot glue fabric bow to back of hat below hatband. Tie 1″ wide ribbon into a bow. Hot glue ribbon bow to fabric bow. Tie remaining ribbon lengths together into a bow; hot glue to 1″ wide bow.
7. For flowers, remove flowers and leaves from stems. Apply 1 coat of gesso to flowers and leaves; allow to dry. Paint flowers and leaves desired colors; allow to dry.
8. To dry brush flowers and leaves, use a dry paintbrush and dip tips of bristles in white paint. Brush tips across paper towels to remove excess paint. Lightly stroke brush across surface of each flower or leaf, highlighting prominent areas; allow to dry.
9. Referring to photo, arrange flowers and leaves on back of hatband above bow; hot glue to secure.

BATTENBURG PAJAMAS (Shown on page 12)

You will need men's short-sleeved short pajamas, a Battenburg lace-trimmed bread cloth and 2 Battenburg lace-trimmed tea towels (see Figs. 1 and 3 for styles of linens we used), two 1″ and two ⅜″ purchased ribbon roses, washable fabric glue, ¾″w lace trim for leg and front openings (see Steps 8 and 10 for amounts), ¾″w lace trim for pocket (see Step 7 for amount), removable fabric marking pen, T-shirt form or cardboard covered with waxed paper, and buttons to coordinate with pajamas and thread to match buttons (optional).

1. Wash, dry, and press pajamas, bread cloth, tea towels, and lace trims. Place T-shirt form inside pajama top.

2. For Battenburg motifs on front of pajama top, cut 2 matching motifs from bread cloth where indicated by grey areas in Fig. 1. Referring to photo, position tops of motifs approximately 2″ from right and left shoulder seams; use fabric marking pen to draw around motifs.

Fig. 1

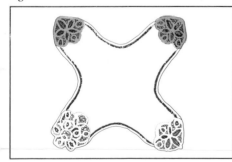

3. Place motifs wrong side up on a flat surface; apply glue to lace tape along outer edge of each motif where indicated by grey line in Fig. 2. Place motifs glue side down at marked areas on pajama top; use fingers to press in place. Allow to dry.

Fig. 2

4. To create openwork area, carefully trim away fabric from behind motifs, cutting close to glued edges.

5. For Battenburg borders on sleeves, cut lace border from each towel as shown by grey area in Fig. 3. With bottom edge of border extending approximately ¼″ beyond bottom edge of each sleeve, refer to photo to center 1 border on each sleeve; use fabric marking pen to draw around borders.

Fig. 3

6. Referring to grey line in Fig. 4 for glue placement, repeat Steps 3 and 4 to apply 1 border to edge of each sleeve.

Fig. 4

7. For pocket trim, measure width of pocket; add 1″. Cut lace the determined measurement. Press ends of lace ½″ to wrong side; glue to secure. Referring to photo, glue lace to pocket.

8. For front opening trim, measure front opening from hem to neck, around neck, and down to opposite hem; add 1″. Cut lace the determined measurement. Press ends of lace ½″ to wrong side; glue to secure. Beginning with 1 pressed end of lace at hemline, glue right side of lace to inside of opening with edge of lace extending ½″ beyond edge of opening.

9. Referring to photo, glue 1″ roses to top and ⅜″ roses to sleeves. Allow to dry. Replace buttons if desired. Remove any visible marking pen lines.

10. For trim on shorts, measure circumference of leg opening; add 1″. Cut lace the determined measurement. Glue right side of lace to inside of leg opening with edge of lace extending ½″ beyond edge of opening. Repeat for remaining leg opening.

11. To launder, follow glue manufacturer's recommendations.

ROSY SLIPPERS
(Shown on page 12)

You will need a pair of house slippers (we used a pair of women's terry scuffs), two 3¾″ dia. purchased crocheted doilies, two 1″ purchased ribbon roses, and thread to match doilies and roses.

1. On wrong side of 1 doily, pinch doily together at center; use thread to tie pinched area together. Knot and trim ends of thread close to knot. Tack pinched area of doily to center top of 1 slipper. Repeat for remaining slipper.

2. Refer to photo and tack 1 rose to center of each doily.

FLOWER BASKET SWEATSHIRT (Shown on page 18)

You will need a sweatshirt, fabrics for appliqués, lightweight fusible interfacing, paper-backed fusible web, 5mm pearls, tracing paper, dimensional fabric paints in squeeze bottles to coordinate with appliqué fabrics and pearls, safety pin, 24″ lengths of desired widths of satin ribbon, see-through pressing cloth, and a T-shirt form or cardboard covered with waxed paper.

1. Use patterns and follow Tracing Patterns, page 124. Cut out patterns.

2. (*Note:* Refer to photo for Steps 2 - 5.) Referring to Diagram, use patterns and follow Making Appliqués, page 124, to fuse 16 leaves, 9 flowers, 1 basket, 1 basket rim, and 1 basket handle to sweatshirt.

3. Follow Steps 2 - 6 of Dimensional Fabric Painting, page 125, to apply paint to appliqués.

4. Use paint to attach 4 pearls to center of each flower. Allow to dry.

5. Tie ribbon lengths into a bow. Use safety pin on wrong side of shirt to pin bow to basket rim.

6. To launder, remove bow and follow paint manufacturer's recommendations.

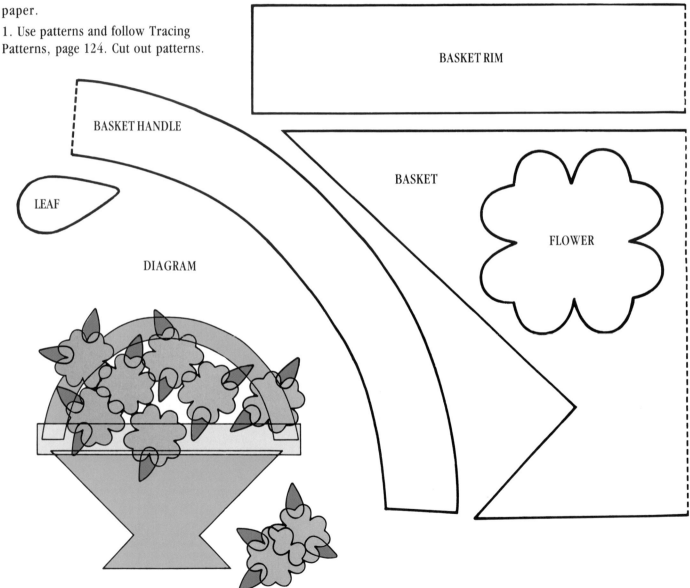

BASKET RIM

BASKET HANDLE

LEAF

DIAGRAM

BASKET

FLOWER

BABY T-SHIRTS (Shown on page 10)

For each T-shirt, you will need desired baby T-shirt, one 3″ square of 10 mesh waste canvas, lightweight non-fusible interfacing, embroidery hoop (optional), tweezers, spray bottle filled with water, masking tape, thread, and embroidery floss (see color key).

Referring to photo for placement, follow Working On Waste Canvas, page 127, to work design on T-shirt. Use 4 strands of floss for Cross Stitch, 1 for Backstitch, and 3 for French Knots.

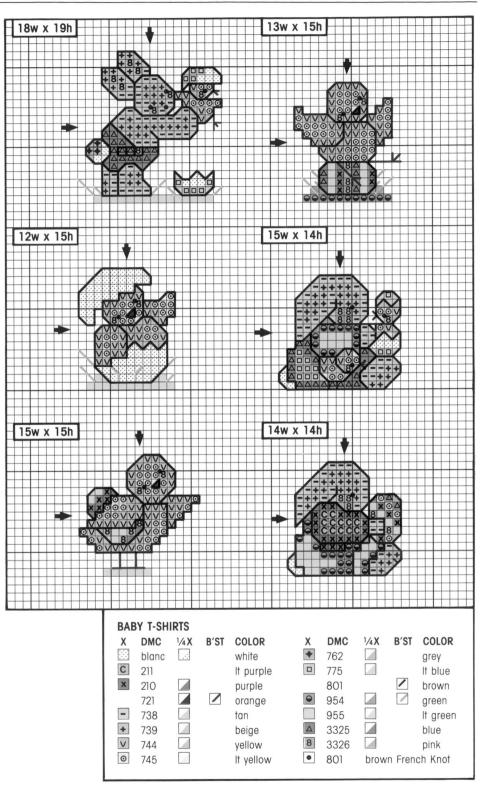

X	DMC	¼X	B'ST	COLOR	X	DMC	¼X	B'ST	COLOR
	blanc			white	✦	762			grey
C	211			lt purple	□	775			lt blue
X	210			purple		801		✓	brown
	721		✓	orange	⊙	954			green
−	738			tan		955			lt green
✛	739			beige	▲	3325			blue
V	744			yellow	8	3326			pink
⊙	745			lt yellow	●	801			brown French Knot

*S*ummer

Summer is take-it-easy time, beckoning us to relax and have fun in the sun. A wardrobe of casual clothes helps us make the most of these long, lazy days. Our playful collection includes comfortable T-shirts, breezy skirts, and colorful cover-ups reflecting all the pleasures of summer — flamboyant flowers, sun-ripened fruits, and a star-spangled Fourth of July. From the beach to the ball park, you'll be set for any summer pastime!

Watermelon Jumper · page 52

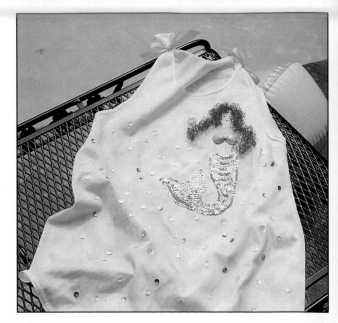

Colorful swim gear makes an afternoon at the pool even more enjoyable! Little girls can choose from two cover-ups — one features a sequined mermaid; the other has bright bikini and beach ball appliqués and a ruffled skirt. A purchased tote bag is appliquéd to match, and dots of shiny paint add pizzazz to a pair of sunglasses.

Mermaid Cover-up, page 57
Bikini Funwear, page 58

Cool Shades Beachwear and
Porthole T-Shirt and Funglasses, page 60

A brilliant yellow sun and vibrant neon sunglasses make this stenciled cover-up a cool way to beat the heat. To shade your face, there's a straw hat with a big, floppy brim.

A ''porthole'' provides a fascinating glimpse of an underwater scene on a child's T-shirt, and matching sunglasses continue the aquatic theme.

*T*hese star-spangled fashions will make a spirited showing on the Fourth of July! A combination of painting techniques was used to decorate the "U.S.A." shirt, while sequins bring lots of sparkle to matching sneakers. Studded with stars and jewels, a bright blue T-shirt adds to the patriotic feeling of the day. For girls, star pins made from wooden cutouts and ribbon can be attached to any outfit, and little boys will get a bang out of the explosive firecracker shirt and cap.

Star-Studded Tee and All-American Shirt and Shoes, page 51

40

Star-Spangled Pins, page 53
'Bang!' T-Shirt and Cap, page 54

*W*hether you plan to spend the day uptown or in the country, you'll love these bold sunflowers! For a city look, fabric dye sticks create an artistic effect on a tailored white shirt. Appliquéd flowers and a picket fence fashioned from ribbon make a chambray jumper as fresh and pretty as a country garden.

Sunflower Shirt, page 51

Sunflower Jumper, page 50

43

Deep red strawberries and rosy watermelons inspire delicious designs for summer tops. A classic chambray shirt is perfect for a touch of embroidery, and trendy tees take to sponge-painting with ease.

For a fun summer ensemble, we borrowed bits and pieces of bright bandanas to trim a denim skirt and coordinating shirt. Paisley motifs from the bandanas wake up the shirt, while the prairie point edging on the skirt makes an old-fashioned statement.

Embroidered Strawberry Shirt, page 54
Fresh Fruit T-Shirts, page 53

Bandana Shirt and Prairie Points Skirt, page 61

45

Little Girls' Sailor Dress, page 55

The whole family can set sail for summer fun in these nautical styles! Little sister will be sitting pretty in a jaunty sailor dress, and big sis will be cool and comfortable in a stenciled jumper. Mom and Dad will be all decked out in these appliquéd shirts. There's one with a life preserver from the "U.S.S. Fun" for her and another with colorful signal flags for him.

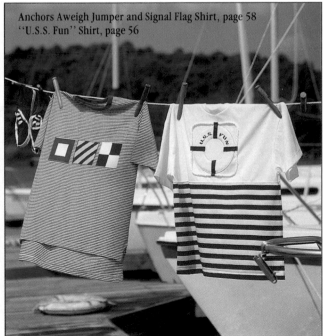

Anchors Aweigh Jumper and Signal Flag Shirt, page 58
"U.S.S. Fun" Shirt, page 56

T*his official-looking "trading card" shirt will make your youngster feel like a pro player! A simple transfer technique is used to apply a color photocopy of a photograph to the shirt.*

Dad will be ready for any summer sport with these cross-stitched caps. Our collection of simple designs includes motifs for fishing, sailing, golfing, and baseball.

Dad's Hats, page 58

SUNFLOWER JUMPER (Shown on page 43)

You will need desired garment (we used a chambray jumper with drop waist and gathered skirt); two 5″ squares of brown fabric for sunflower centers; eight 5″ squares of green solid or print fabric for leaves; thirty-six 3″ squares of gold fabric for petals; paper-backed fusible web; 1 yd of green single-fold bias tape; 2¼ yds of 1½″w white grosgrain ribbon; 22½″ of 1″w white grosgrain ribbon; white, green, and brown thread; brown buttons in assorted sizes; item(s) to transfer patterns to fabric (see Transferring Patterns, page 124); rip-away backing or medium weight paper; see-through pressing cloth; glue stick; compass; and tracing paper.

1. Wash, dry, and press garment, fabrics, and trims.
2. (*Note:* Refer to photo and Diagram for Steps 2 - 5.) For stems, cut one 23″ length and one 9½″ length from bias tape. Press 1 end (bottom) of 23″ length ½″ to wrong side. Place lengths on skirt; glue to secure. Stitching close to edges, sew lengths to skirt.
3. For fence rail, press 1 end of 1″ wide ribbon ½″ to wrong side. With pressed end of ribbon at skirt seamline, glue ribbon to skirt. Stitching close to edges, sew ribbon to skirt.
4. For fence pickets, cut nine 8¼″ lengths from 1½″ wide ribbon. Fold 1 ribbon length in half lengthwise. Using a ¼″ seam allowance, sew across 1 end. Turn right side out to form a point (Fig. 1); press. Press remaining end ½″ to wrong side. Repeat for remaining lengths.

Fig. 1

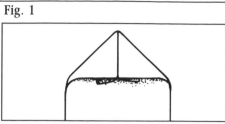

5. Place pickets, seam side down, on skirt; glue in place. Stitching close to edges, sew pickets to skirt.
6. For leaves, follow manufacturer's instructions to fuse web to wrong sides of 4 green fabric squares. Fuse squares to wrong sides of remaining 4 squares.
7. Follow Tracing Patterns and Transferring Patterns, page 124, to transfer leaf pattern onto 1 fabric square. Referring to pattern, stitch on solid lines. Trim fabric to ⅛″ from stitching line. For tuck at base of leaf, refer to pattern and fold leaf along dashed line. Match fold to dotted line. Securely tack tuck at base of leaf. Repeat for remaining fabric squares.
8. Referring to Diagram, position leaves along stems. Tack center back and base of each leaf in place.

9. Using petal pattern and brown thread, repeat Steps 6 and 7 to make 18 petals from gold fabric squares.
10. Following manufacturer's instructions, fuse web to wrong sides of brown fabric squares. Do not remove paper backing. Use compass to mark one 3″ diameter circle on 1 fabric square and one 3½″ diameter circle on remaining fabric square; cut out.
11. For each flower, remove paper backing from 1 circle. Place circle, web side up, on ironing board. Overlapping petal edges, place bases of 9 petals ¼″ inside edge of circle. Being careful not to touch exposed web, use tip of iron to fuse petals to back of circle.
12. Follow Step 5 of Making Appliqués, page 124, and Machine Appliquéing, page 125, to appliqué flower centers to skirt.
13. Sew buttons to centers of flowers.

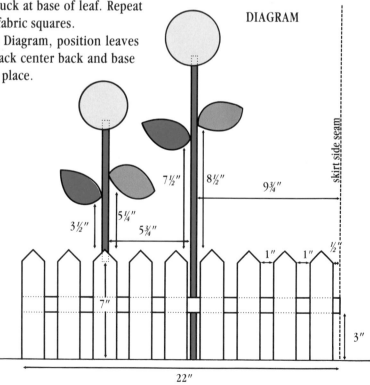

DIAGRAM

SUNFLOWER SHIRT (Shown on page 42)

You will need a shirt (we used a men's white cotton-blend dress shirt), Pentel® Fabricfun™ Pastel Dye Sticks (available in sets at craft stores), green and brown permanent felt-tip pens with fine points, T-shirt form or cardboard covered with waxed paper, item(s) to transfer patterns to shirt (see Transferring Patterns, page 124), and tracing paper.

1. Wash, dry, and press shirt.
2. (*Note*: Refer to photo for Steps 2 - 5.) Use sunflower and leaf patterns and follow Tracing Patterns and Transferring Patterns, page 124, to transfer patterns to shirt.
3. Insert T-shirt form in shirt. Following dye stick manufacturer's instructions, color sunflower and leaves the following colors:
   Center - lt orange, gold, and brown
   Front petals - yellow shaded with
      lt orange and gold
   Back petals - lt orange shaded with
      brown
   Leaves - lt green shaded with
      dk green and brown
4. Heat-set designs according to dye stick manufacturer's instructions.
5. Use brown pen to draw the following: a heavy outline and a ¼" wide zigzag line around center of flower, circular swirls in center of flower, outlines of petals, and veins in petals. Use green pen to outline leaves and to draw veins in leaves.
6. To launder, follow dye stick manufacturer's recommendations.

ALL-AMERICAN SHIRT AND SHOES (Shown on page 40)

For shirt, you will need a T-shirt, 5"h Roman lettering stencils, eighteen ¾"w gold star jewels, bright gold glitter and antique gold glitter dimensional fabric paint in squeeze bottles, 1¼ yds of red string sequins, 1¼ yds of white string sequins, removable tape (optional), and T-shirt form or cardboard covered with waxed paper.
For shoes, you will need a pair of white canvas tennis shoes, ¾"w gold star jewels, red string sequins, and white string sequins.
You will also need blue fabric paint, washable jewel glue, stencil brush, and paper towels.

SHIRT
1. Follow paint manufacturers' recommendations to wash, dry, and press shirt.
2. (*Note:* Refer to photo for Steps 2 - 4.) Spacing letters ½" apart, use blue paint and follow Steps 4 and 5 of Stenciling, page 126, to stencil ''USA'' on shirt.
3. (*Note*: To prevent sequin string from unraveling when cut, apply a small amount of glue to area to be cut; allow to dry. Cut apart at glued area.) For flag, cut one 15" length and two 10" lengths of red sequins. Cut two 15" lengths and one 10" length of white sequins. Arrange stars and sequin lengths on top of stenciled letters; glue to secure. Allow to dry.
4. (*Note:* Refer to Steps 3 - 7 of Dimensional Fabric Painting, page 125, for Step 4.) For center of each starburst, use thick lines of bright gold paint to draw curved lines out from a center point. For remaining bright gold and antique gold lines, press tip of bottle firmly onto fabric and drag tip outward from center of starburst to create flat lines.

SHOES
1. (*Note:* Refer to photo for all steps.) To paint shoes, use blue paint and stencil brush and apply paint lightly in a stamping motion.
2. Trimming sequin strings as necessary, glue 1 length of white and 2 lengths of red sequins to each shoe. Allow to dry.
3. Glue stars to toes of shoes. Allow to dry.

STAR-STUDDED TEE
(Shown on page 40)

You will need a T-shirt, gold iron-on Hot Dots™ (available at craft stores), ¼" dia. and ⅜" dia. gold nail heads, 1"w and 1¾"w gold star appliqués, ⅝" dia. red jewel stones, and washable jewel glue.

1. Wash, dry, and press shirt.
2. (*Note:* Refer to photo for Steps 2 - 4.) Cut eight 6" long strips of Hot Dots™. Following manufacturer's instructions, apply dots to shirt.
3. Following manufacturer's instructions, attach nail heads to shirt.
4. Glue jewels and appliqués to shirt. Allow to dry.
5. To launder, follow glue manufacturer's recommendations.

Note: This project is suitable for Misses sizes.

You will need painter's overalls, 45"w ticking fabric for skirt (see Step 3 for amount), 1 yd of 45"w pink print fabric for appliqués and ties, one 3½ yd long 2"w bias strip of lt green fabric for narrow ruffle and one 6 yd long 4"w strip of dk green print fabric for wide ruffle (pieced as necessary), thread to match fabrics, seam ripper, lightweight fusible interfacing, paper-backed fusible web, tracing paper, rip-away backing or medium weight paper, see-through pressing cloth, small round paintbrush, and black dimensional fabric paint in squeeze bottle.

1. Wash, dry, and press overalls and fabric pieces.

2. For bib, use seam ripper to remove overalls bib from front of overalls along seamline at waist; press seam allowance flat. Cut off back of overalls even with front of overalls. Discard bottom half of overalls.

3. For skirt pieces, measure from waistline of bib to desired hemline. Cut 2 pieces of ticking fabric 43" wide by the determined length.

4. (*Note:* Use a ½" seam allowance for Steps 4 - 16 unless otherwise indicated.) Matching right sides and raw edges, place skirt pieces together. Referring to Fig. 1 and beginning 7" below top edge of skirt, sew each side seam. Press seams open. Turn right side out.

Fig. 1

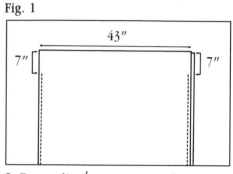

5. For appliqués, use watermelon pattern (shown in pink on page 53) and follow Tracing Patterns, page 124. Cut out pattern.

6. Cut one 26" x 45" piece from pink fabric. Follow Steps 2 and 3 of Making Appliqués, page 124, to make 12 watermelon appliqués.

7. Referring to Fig. 2, follow Step 5 of Making Appliqués, page 124, to fuse 6 appliqués to bottom front of skirt. Repeat for back of skirt.

Fig. 2

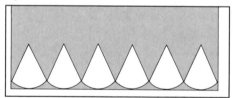

8. To appliqué straight edges only of each appliqué, follow Machine Appliquéing, page 125. Referring to Fig. 3, trim away excess skirt fabric along bottom curves of appliqués.

Fig. 3

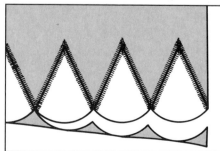

9. For narrow ruffle, match right sides and short edges and fold 2" wide fabric strip in half. Sew short edges together to form a loop. Press seam open.

10. Matching wrong sides and raw edges, fold ruffle fabric in half; press. Baste ½" and ¼" from raw edge. Pull basting threads, drawing up gathers to fit along bottom edge of skirt.

11. Matching right sides and raw edges, pin ruffle to bottom edge of skirt. Baste ruffle to skirt.

12. For wide ruffle, use 4" wide fabric strip and repeat Steps 9 - 11.

13. Stitch ruffles to skirt. Remove all visible basting threads and trim seam allowance to ⅛"; press seam allowance toward skirt.

14. For top of skirt, use a pin to mark top front edge of skirt ½" from each side edge. Baste between pins ½" and ¼" from top edge. Pull basting threads, gathering area between pins to same length as raw edge of bib.

15. With right sides together and matching raw edges, center bottom edge of bib along top edge of skirt; pin in place. Sew bib to skirt. Press seam allowance toward skirt. Press remaining edge at each side of skirt front to wrong side of bib; whipstitch top edge of skirt front to bib.

16. For skirt back, repeat Steps 14 and 15.

17. For ties at waist, cut two 4" x 44" strips from pink fabric. Matching right sides, fold 1 strip in half lengthwise. Using a ¼" seam allowance and leaving an opening for turning, sew raw edges together. Cut corners diagonally, turn right side out, and press. Sew final closure by hand. Repeat for remaining tie.

WATERMELON JUMPER

(continued)

18. Referring to Fig. 4, center 1 tie on back of overalls. Matching seam of tie to bottom edge of bib, pin in place. Sew tie in place (Fig. 4). Repeat for remaining tie on front of bib.

Fig. 4

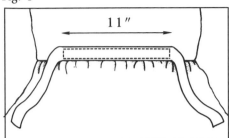

19. Referring to photo, use paintbrush and dimensional paint to paint seeds on watermelons. Allow to dry.

20. To launder, follow paint manufacturer's recommendations.

STAR-SPANGLED PINS

(Shown on page 41)

You will need 2"w wooden star cutouts; blue spray paint; high gloss clear acrylic spray; ⅛"w blue, red, and gold metallic curling ribbon; 1" long pin backs; and craft glue.

1. Paint stars blue; allow to dry. Spray stars with 1 coat of acrylic spray; allow to dry.

2. For each pin, cut five 5" lengths each of red, gold, and blue ribbon. Apply a large flat dot of glue to back of star. Refer to photo to position 1 of each color ribbon between 2 points of star; repeat for remaining lengths. Allow to dry. Glue pin back to back of star over ribbon ends; allow to dry. Use scissors to curl ends of ribbon.

FRESH FRUIT T-SHIRTS   (Shown on page 44)

For each shirt, you will need a washed, dried, and pressed T-shirt; cellulose sponges; tracing paper; washable fabric glue; T-shirt form or cardboard covered with waxed paper; foam brushes; and permanent felt-tip pen with fine point.

For strawberry shirt, you will also need 2 yds of ⅛"w satin ribbon; white, red, black, and green fabric paint; white and yellow dimensional fabric paint in squeeze bottles; green permanent felt-tip pen with fine point; and removable fabric marking pen.

For watermelon shirt, you will also need pink, lt green, green, and yellow fabric paint; ¼"w white rickrack; and buttons.

STRAWBERRY SHIRT

1. Use strawberry, flower, leaf, strawberry cap, and border patterns and follow Tracing Patterns, page 124. Cut out patterns.

2. Use removable fabric marking pen to draw an 11¼" x 12½" rectangle on shirt front.

3. (*Note*: Refer to photo for Steps 3 - 7.) Beginning border at inside top left corner of drawn rectangle, use patterns and fabric paint and follow Steps 2 - 5 of Sponge Painting, page 126, to paint design the following colors:

    Border squares - black
    Strawberries - red
    Flowers - white
    Strawberry caps and leaves - green

4. Use green pen to outline strawberry caps and leaves, to draw veins on leaves, and to draw dashed lines connecting strawberries, leaves, and flowers.

5. For flowers, use dimensional paint and follow Steps 3 - 6 of Dimensional Fabric Painting, page 125, to outline

flowers in white and to paint flower centers yellow.

6. For ribbon border, cut a 1½ yd length from ribbon. Glue ribbon to shirt ½" from edge of painted design, trimming ends if necessary.

7. Cut remaining ribbon in half. Tie each length into a bow; trim ends. Glue bows to bottom corners of ribbon border.

8. Remove fabric marking pen lines.

9. To launder, follow paint and glue manufacturers' recommendations.

WATERMELON SHIRT

1. Use watermelon and rind patterns (shown in green) and follow Tracing Patterns, page 124. Cut out patterns.

2. (*Note*: Refer to photo for Steps 2 - 5.) Using watermelon pattern and pink paint, follow Steps 2 - 5 of Sponge Painting, page 126, to paint watermelon designs on shirt.

3. For watermelon rinds and borders along bottom edges of sleeves and shirt, follow Step 2 of Sponge Painting, page 126, to cut 3 rind pieces from sponge. Follow Steps 4 and 5 of Sponge Painting to alternately stamp green and yellow rinds and borders. Use lt green paint and lightly stamp over yellow paint.

4. Cut pieces of rickrack to fit along rinds of watermelon slices; glue to secure. Allow to dry.

5. Arrange buttons on shirt; glue to secure. Allow to dry.

6. To launder, follow paint and glue manufacturers' recommendations.

EMBROIDERED STRAWBERRY SHIRT

(Shown on page 44)

You will need a shirt (we used a button-front chambray shirt), tracing paper, hot-iron transfer pencil or other item(s) to transfer pattern to shirt (see Transferring Patterns, page 124), embroidery floss (see color key), and embroidery hoop.

1. Referring to photo, follow Tracing Patterns and Transferring Patterns, page 124, to transfer pattern to shirt.
2. (*Note:* Embroidery Stitch Diagrams are shown on pages 127 and 128.) Follow stitch key and color key and use 2 strands of floss to work design.

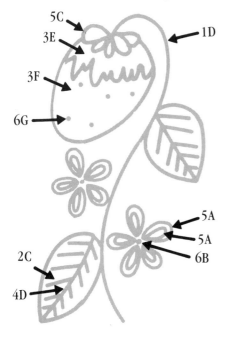

STITCH KEY	COLOR KEY
1 - Stem Stitch	A - white
2 - Satin Stitch	B - yellow
3 - Brick Stitch	C - lt green
4 - Fern Stitch	D - dk green
5 - Lazy Daisy	E - pink
6 - French Knot	F - red
	G - black

"BANG!" T-SHIRT AND CAP (Shown on page 41)

For shirt, you will need a T-shirt; fabrics for appliqués; dimensional fabric paint in squeeze bottles to coordinate with appliqué fabrics; pewter opalescent, red glitter, gold glitter, and silver glitter dimensional paint in squeeze bottles; tracing paper; paper-backed fusible web; lightweight fusible interfacing; see-through pressing cloth; T-shirt form or cardboard covered with waxed paper; and removable fabric marking pen.

For cap, you will need a cap, two 1¾" x 2½" strips of fabric for firecrackers, two 2½" lengths of middy braid, assorted sequins, dimensional fabric paint in squeeze bottle, removable fabric marking pen, and fabric glue.

SHIRT

1. Trace firecracker and firecracker top patterns, this page, onto tracing paper; cut out.
2. (*Note:* Refer to photo for Steps 2 - 5.) Use patterns and follow Making Appliqués, page 124.
3. Use fabric marking pen to write "Bang!" on shirt and to draw fuses on firecrackers.
4. Follow Steps 2 - 5 of Dimensional Fabric Painting, page 125, to paint over drawn lines and edges of appliqués. Allow to dry.
5. For fire around fuse of each firecracker, use red glitter paint to draw a star shape around end of fuse. Referring to Fig. 1, drag tip of bottle outward through wet paint to spread paint into thin lines; allow to dry. Repeat with gold glitter then silver glitter paint.

Fig. 1

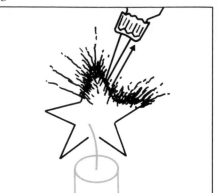

6. With shirt lying flat, allow paint to dry following paint manufacturer's recommendations for drying time.
7. To launder, follow paint manufacturer's recommendations.

CAP

1. Refer to photo and use fabric marking pen to write "Bang!" on cap.
2. Follow Steps 3 - 6 of Dimensional Fabric Painting, page 125, to paint over drawn lines.
3. For each firecracker, fray 1 end of braid ½". Place braid on wrong side of fabric strip along 1 short edge with frayed end extending beyond fabric. Glue to secure. Beginning at glued edge, roll fabric strip into a tube (Fig. 1); glue to secure.

Fig. 1

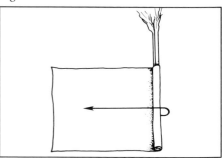

4. Refer to photo to glue firecrackers and sequins to cap.

LITTLE GIRLS' SAILOR DRESS (Shown on page 46)

Note: This project is suitable for Toddler Girls' sizes.

You will need a T-shirt, fabric for collar and skirt, a 4½" square of fabric for dickey, middy braid for collar and skirt trim, 2½" of ⅞"w grosgrain ribbon, 2 buttons for sleeves, thread to match shirt and fabric, fabric marking pencil, washable fabric glue, and a purchased 1½"h anchor appliqué.

1. Wash, dry, and press shirt, fabric, ribbon, and braid.

2. Try shirt on child and mark with a pin 3" below natural waistline. Place shirt on a flat surface and use pencil to draw a line across shirt at pin mark; cut off bottom of shirt along drawn line.

3. For skirt, measure circumference of bottom of shirt and multiply by 2½. Cut a strip of fabric 7" wide by the determined measurement (pieced as necessary). For braid trim, cut 2 lengths of braid the determined measurement.

4. Matching right sides and short edges, use a ½" seam allowance to sew short edges of fabric strip together to form a loop. Press seam open.

5. For hem, press 1 long raw edge ½" to wrong side; press 1" to wrong side again. Stitch in place. Turn right side out.

6. Referring to photo and overlapping ends of trim at seam, glue 1 braid length over stitching line at hem; glue remaining length ½" from bottom of skirt.

7. Machine baste ½" and ¼" away from remaining raw edge of skirt. Pull basting threads, gathering skirt to fit bottom of shirt.

8. Matching right sides and raw edges, use a ½" seam allowance to stitch skirt to shirt. Press seam allowance toward shirt. Topstitch on shirt ⅜" and ⅛" from skirt seam.

9. For collar, measure length of shirt from shoulder to bottom of shirt. Cut 2 strips of fabric 6½" wide by the determined measurement. Cut 2 lengths of braid the determined measurement; cut two 3¾" lengths of braid.

10. Matching right sides, press 1 strip in half lengthwise. Using a ½" seam allowance, sew along long raw edge and 1 short edge. Cut corners diagonally, turn right side out, and press. Repeat for remaining strip.

11. For left collar piece, place 1 collar piece on a flat surface with long sewn edge at left and short raw edge at top. Center 1 short braid length on collar piece ¼" from bottom edge; glue in place. Center 1 long braid length ¼" from right edge; glue in place. Fold ends of braid to back of collar piece; glue in place. Allow to dry.

12. For right collar piece, place remaining collar piece on a flat surface with long sewn edge at right and short raw edge at top. Repeat Step 11 to glue remaining lengths of braid to bottom and left edges of collar piece.

13. For tucks in collar pieces, match right sides and fold left collar piece in half lengthwise; place a pin through all layers of fabric ½" from folded edge as shown in Fig. 1. Without removing pin, unfold collar piece and press fold of tuck toward long pressed edge. Baste ½" from raw edge of collar piece to secure. Repeat for right collar piece.

Fig. 1

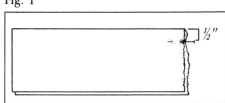

14. With right side of collar piece facing right side of back of shirt, match basting line on right collar piece to right shoulder seam on shirt (Fig. 2); pin in place. Sew collar piece to shirt along basting line. Press collar piece to front of shirt and remove any visible basting threads. Repeat for left collar piece.

Fig. 2

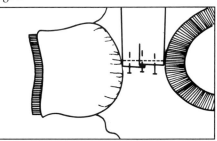

15. (*Note:* Refer to photo for Steps 15 - 17.) Cross collar pieces and pinch together. Wrap ribbon length around pinched area and glue ends of ribbon to secure. Allow to dry.

16. With wrong sides together, press dickey piece in half diagonally. Glue raw edges together. Place dickey behind collar with point behind ribbon and pressed edge at top; glue to shirt. Glue ribbon loop to dickey. Allow to dry.

17. Glue anchor appliqué to dickey; glue 1 button to top of each sleeve near hem. Allow to dry.

18. To launder, follow glue manufacturer's recommendations.

"U.S.S. FUN" SHIRT (Shown on page 47)

You will need a shirt (we used a purchased red and white striped T-shirt with white yoke and sleeves), one 9″ square of fabric for appliqué, two 9″ squares of fusible craft batting, lightweight fusible interfacing, paper-backed fusible web, rip-away backing or medium weight paper, 20″ of ⅝″w grosgrain ribbon, 30″ of ⅜″ dia. cotton cord, desired color fabric paint, thread to match fabric and ribbon, compass, tracing paper, small stencil brush, paper towels, removable tape (optional), purchased ½″h lettering stencils, washable fabric glue, and removable fabric marking pen.

1. Follow Steps 1 and 2 of Making Appliqués, page 124, to prepare garment and fabric for appliqué.
2. For life preserver pattern, cut a 10″ square from tracing paper and fold in half from top to bottom and again from left to right. Use compass to draw lines on paper as shown in Fig. 1. Cutting through all layers, cut out pattern along pencil lines. Unfold pattern and lay flat.

Fig. 1

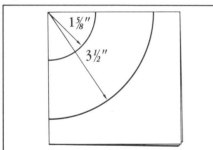

3. Use pattern and cut 1 life preserver from fabric and 2 from batting. Trim 1 batting piece ⅛″ inside cut edges. Trim remaining batting piece ⅜″ inside cut edges.
4. For placement lines, place pattern on shirt. Use fabric marking pen to draw around pattern; remove pattern. Center and fuse smallest batting piece inside placement lines. Center and fuse remaining batting piece over small batting piece. Matching placement lines and edges of fabric appliqué, fuse appliqué to shirt.
5. Follow Machine Appliquéing, page 125, to stitch appliqué to shirt.
6. For bands on life preserver, cut ribbon into four 5″ lengths. Press 1 end of each length ½″ to 1 side (wrong side). Referring to photo for placement, glue folded end of each ribbon piece along inner opening of preserver.
7. For rope trim, apply glue to ¾″ of each end of cord; allow to dry. Cut off ½″ of each glued area. Glue cut ends of cord together to form a ring; allow to dry.
8. Referring to photo, place rope ring around appliqué with glued area at center bottom of design. Fold remaining end of each ribbon piece over and behind rope trim and tack in place (Fig. 2). Use glue to secure rope trim to shirt front. Allow to dry.

Fig. 2

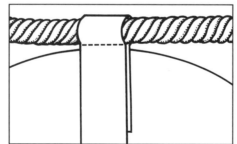

9. Referring to photo, use lettering stencils and follow Steps 5 - 7 of Stenciling, page 126, to stencil "U.S.S. Fun" on appliqué.
10. To launder, follow paint and glue manufacturers' recommendations.

TRADING CARD SHIRT
(Shown on page 48)

You will need a T-shirt, a 5″ x 7″ sports photograph, a 4″ x 6″ piece of white paper for baseball label, a 5¼″ x 8″ piece of colored paper for background of trading card, an 8½″ x 11″ sheet of white paper, desired rub-on letters, burnisher (available at art supply stores) or small crochet hook, Sloman's® Stitchless Fabric Glue and Transfer Medium, dimensional fabric paint in squeeze bottle to match colored paper, green and white fabric paint, red and black permanent felt-tip pens with fine points, removable tape, waxed paper, foam brush, removable fabric marking pen, T-shirt form or cardboard covered with waxed paper, see-through pressing cloth, brayer or rolling pin, and paintbrushes.

Note: After the trading card is complete (Steps 2 - 4), a reverse image color photocopy using a color photocopy machine will need to be made to complete project. This service is available at most photocopy stores.

1. Wash, dry, and press shirt according to paint manufacturers' recommendations.
2. For trading card, center colored paper on 8½″ x 11″ sheet of white paper; use loops of tape to secure. Trim any white borders from photo. Center photo on colored paper with top edge of photo ¼″ from 1 short edge of paper; use loops of tape to secure.
3. Place 4″ x 6″ piece of white paper over baseball label pattern and use a pencil to lightly trace grey lines. Use red pen to trace baseball laces. Use black pen to trace remaining lines of pattern. Using pencil lines as guides to keep letters straight, use tip of burnisher to rub letters onto label to form desired

words. Carefully erase pencil lines. Cut out label.

4. Referring to photo, page 48, center label over bottom of sports photo; use loops of tape to secure.

5. Have a reverse image color photocopy of trading card made. Referring to photo, cut out photocopy along edge of colored background.

6. Place T-shirt form inside shirt. Place photocopy right side down on front of shirt and use fabric marking pen to draw around photocopy.

7. To transfer photocopy to shirt, apply an even coat of glue to front of photocopy so that image barely shows through glue. Without touching glue, place photocopy glue side down on shirt inside pen lines.

8. Cover photocopy with waxed paper. Firmly roll brayer over copy to remove any air bubbles. Remove waxed paper and allow photocopy to dry for 24 hours.

9. Heat-set transfer using pressing cloth and a hot dry iron.

10. To remove paper from transfer, brush a liberal amount of warm water over photocopy; allow water to stand for several minutes. Working from center to outside edges, use fingers to gently roll a thin layer of paper away from transfer (transfer will appear cloudy). Adding water as necessary, repeat process until transfer is as clear as original photocopy. Allow to dry.

11. To seal transfer, mix 1 part glue to 1 part water. Apply a thin coat of glue mixture over transfer. Allow to dry.

12. Referring to Fig. 1, use fabric marking pen to draw baseball diamond around transfer. Paint diamond green; allow to dry. Referring to photo, use white paint to paint bases and lines $\frac{1}{4}''$ inside diamond; allow to dry. Using dimensional paint, follow Steps 2 - 6 of

Dimensional Fabric Painting, page 125, to outline trading card.

Fig. 1

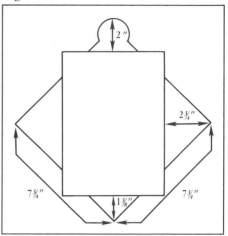

13. To launder, follow glue and paint manufacturers' recommendations.

MERMAID COVER-UP   (Shown on page 38)

You will need a men's tank top T-shirt; two 18" lengths of $\frac{5}{8}''$w satin ribbon; curly doll hair (available at craft stores); three 1" dia. shell-shaped buttons with shanks removed; tracing paper; item(s) to transfer pattern to shirt (see Transferring Patterns, page 124); paintbrushes; washable jewel glue; $2\frac{1}{2}$ yds of green string sequins; assorted loose sequins; blue spray fabric dye (available at craft stores); thread to match shirt and hair; peach, dk pink, lt pink, white, and green fabric paint; black permanent felt-tip pen with fine point; and T-shirt form or cardboard covered with waxed paper.

1. Wash, dry, and press shirt according to paint and dye manufacturers'

recommendations. Insert T-shirt form into shirt.

2. (*Note*: Refer to photo for Steps 2 - 10.) For waves, follow manufacturer's instructions and use spray dye to spray wavy horizontal lines on shirt. Allow to dry.

3. To transfer pattern to shirt, follow Tracing Patterns and Transferring Patterns, page 124.

4. Paint mermaid the following colors:
    Upper body - peach
    Eyes - green with white highlights
    Lips - dk pink
    Cheeks - lt pink
Allow to dry.

5. Use permanent pen to draw over outlines of eyes, eyelashes, nose, and mouth.

6. Glue 2 shell buttons to upper body; glue 1 shell button to hand. Allow to dry.

7. Glue string sequins along outline of lower body. Glue remaining string sequins to shirt, filling in outlined area. Allow to dry.

8. Glue loose sequins randomly over waves; allow to dry.

9. For hair, cut one 12" bunch of hair. Arrange hair on mermaid and tack in place.

10. For each shoulder tie, stitch shoulder strap together 2" below shoulder seam. Tie 1 ribbon length into a bow around stitching line; trim ends.

11. To launder, remove bows and follow paint, dye, and glue manufacturers' recommendations.

BIKINI FUNWEAR (Shown on page 38)

You will need a T-shirt for cover-up; a tote bag; sunglasses; fabrics for appliqués; fabric for ruffle; 1"w grosgrain ribbon for ruffle trim; dimensional fabric paints in squeeze bottles to match or coordinate with appliqué fabrics; lightweight fusible interfacing; paper-backed fusible web; tracing paper; see-through pressing cloth; T-shirt form or cardboard covered with waxed paper; and thread to match shirt, ruffle, and ribbon.

1. For patterns, trace bikini top and bottom, outline of beach ball, and grey area of beach ball onto separate pieces of tracing paper; cut out.
2. (*Note:* Refer to photo for Steps 2 and 3.) Use patterns and appliqué fabrics and follow Making Appliqués, page 124, to apply appliqués to shirt and tote bag.
3. Follow Steps 2 - 6 of Dimensional Fabric Painting, page 125, to outline appliqués, paint centers of beach balls, and paint ties on bikini bottoms.
4. For ruffle on shirt, measure circumference of shirt hem and multiply by 2½. Cut a strip of fabric 4½" wide

by determined measurement (pieced as necessary). Cut 1 length of ribbon determined measurement.
5. Press 1 long edge of ruffle strip ½" to right side. Matching right sides and short edges, use a ½" seam allowance to sew short edges of ruffle strip together to form a loop. Press seam open. Turn right side out.
6. Press 1 end of ribbon ½" to wrong side. With unpressed end of ribbon at seamline and with 1 long edge of ribbon even with pressed edge of ruffle, pin ribbon to right side of ruffle. Stitch along each long edge of ribbon.
7. Baste ½" and ¼" from remaining raw edge of ruffle. Pull basting threads, gathering ruffle to fit hem of shirt. With right sides facing and matching shirt hem to raw edge of ruffle, use a ½" seam allowance to sew ruffle to shirt. Press seam allowance toward shirt. Topstitch on shirt close to seam.
8. To launder, follow paint manufacturer's recommendations.
9. For sunglasses, paint frames with dots of paint. Allow to dry.

ANCHORS AWEIGH JUMPER (Shown on page 47)

You will need desired garment (we used a cotton knit shorts jumper), fabric paint, acetate for stencils (available at craft or art supply stores), craft knife, stencil brushes, cutting mat or a thick layer of newspapers, paper towels, removable tape (optional), cardboard covered with waxed paper, and permanent felt-tip pen with fine point.

Referring to photo, use anchor pattern and follow Stenciling, page 126, to stencil design on garment, reversing stencils if desired.

SIGNAL FLAG SHIRT
(Shown on page 47)

You will need a T-shirt; white, yellow, red, and blue fabric for appliqués; lightweight fusible interfacing; thread to match fabrics; see-through pressing cloth; paper-backed fusible web; removable fabric marking pen; and rip-away backing or medium weight paper.

1. Follow Steps 1 and 2 of Making Appliqués, page 124.
2. Cut one 4" square each from blue, yellow, white, and red fabrics. Cut one 2" square from white and two 2" squares from red fabric.
3. (*Note:* Refer to photo for Steps 3 - 5.) Follow Step 5 of Making Appliqués, page 124, to fuse 4" blue, yellow, and white squares to shirt. Fuse 2" white square to center of blue square. Fuse 2" red squares to 4" white square.
4. For red stripes on yellow square, use fabric marking pen to draw a line diagonally across center of remaining red square. Measuring from center line and working toward 1 corner, draw 4 more lines ½" apart on square. Cut along drawn lines. Arrange 4 red pieces on yellow square; trim to fit. Fuse in place. Discard remaining red pieces.
5. To secure appliqués, follow Machine Appliquéing, page 125.

DAD'S HATS
(Shown on page 49)

For each hat, you will need a Crafter's Pride® Sportsman Hat (14 ct) and embroidery floss (see color key).

Work desired design on front of hat, using 2 strands of floss for Cross Stitch and 1 for Backstitch.

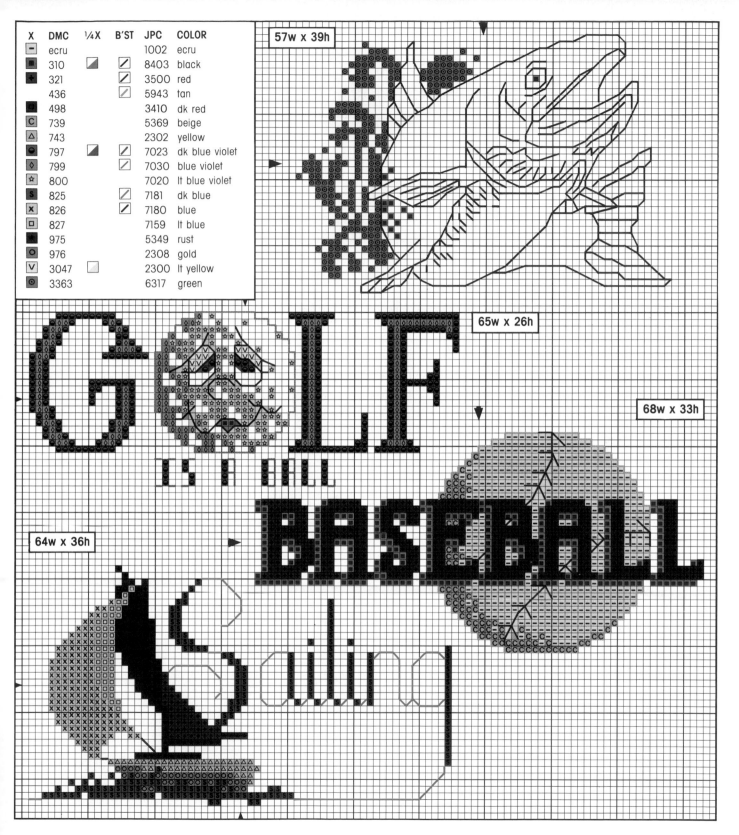

X	DMC	¼X	B'ST	JPC	COLOR
−	ecru			1002	ecru
■	310	◩	◪	8403	black
✚	321		◪	3500	red
	436		◪	5943	tan
▣	498			3410	dk red
C	739			5369	beige
△	743			2302	yellow
◉	797	◩	◪	7023	dk blue violet
◇	799		◪	7030	blue violet
☆	800			7020	lt blue violet
S	825		◪	7181	dk blue
X	826		◪	7180	blue
▢	827			7159	lt blue
★	975			5349	rust
O	976			2308	gold
V	3047	◨		2300	lt yellow
◎	3363			6317	green

57w x 39h

65w x 26h

68w x 33h

64w x 36h

COOL SHADES BEACHWEAR (Shown on page 39)

You will need a cover-up (we used a knit cover-up with elastic waist); a straw hat; iridescent glitter, yellow, pink, orange, green, and black fabric paint; acetate for stencils (available at craft or art supply stores); stencil brushes; flat paintbrushes; toothbrush; cutting mat or a thick layer of newspapers; permanent felt-tip pen with fine point; removable tape (optional); paper towels; craft knife; removable fabric marking pen; T-shirt form or cardboard covered with waxed paper; black, green, and bright pink dimensional fabric paint in squeeze bottles; and orange and yellow shoelaces.

1. Wash, dry, and press cover-up according to paint manufacturers' recommendations.
2. (*Note:* Refer to photo for Steps 2 - 10.) Insert T-shirt form in cover-up. For sun, use fabric marking pen to draw ¼ of a circle on left shoulder. Staying inside shoulder and armhole seams, paint sun yellow. Allow to dry.
3. Using orange paint for sun rays, pink or green fabric paint for sunglasses frames, and black fabric paint for lenses, follow Steps 2 - 7 of Stenciling, page 126, to stencil sun rays, frames, then lenses on cover-up.
4. Paint a light coat of iridescent glitter over sun and sun rays; allow to dry.

5. To spatter cover-up, cut pieces of scrap paper slightly larger than painted designs. Place paper over designs. Use yellow and orange paint and follow Step 2 of Spatter Painting, page 126.
6. For designs on sun, use fabric marking pen to draw designs along edge of sun. Follow Steps 3 - 7 of Dimensional Fabric Painting, page 125, to paint over drawn lines.
7. For belt, tie shoelaces around waistline.
8. For hat, paint a 1¾"w yellow strip around hat brim. Allow to dry.
9. Repeat Step 6 to paint designs on hat.
10. Tie shoelaces into a bow around crown of hat.

PORTHOLE T-SHIRT AND FUNGLASSES (Shown on page 39)

You will need a T-shirt, sunglasses, 10" square of medium weight clear vinyl (available at fabric stores), 10" square of silver metallic fabric for appliqué, 1"w hook and clasp belt buckle, two ¼" dia. silver buttons with shanks removed, silver metallic sewing thread, paper-backed fusible web, lightweight fusible interfacing, rip-away backing or medium weight paper, washable fabric glue, compass, removable fabric marking pen, see-through pressing cloth, tracing paper, all-purpose household cement, and gold seed beads and other items to decorate appliqué and glasses (we used plastic aquarium grasses and figures, coin charms, shells, and fish buttons.)

1. Wash, dry, and press shirt and fabric.
2. For appliqué pattern, cut a 10" square from tracing paper and fold in half from top to bottom and again from left to right. Use compass to draw lines on paper as shown in Fig. 1.

Cutting through all layers, cut out pattern along pencil lines. Unfold pattern and lay flat.

Fig. 1

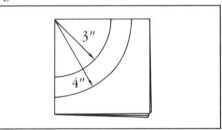

3. For placement lines, place pattern on shirt. Use fabric marking pen to draw around pattern; remove pattern. Arrange decorative items, except seed beads, inside inner circle on shirt front; glue to secure. Allow to dry.
4. Cut a 7" dia. circle from vinyl. Center vinyl circle over drawn inner circle. Leaving an opening at top of circle to insert beads, glue edge of circle to shirt; allow to dry. Insert beads through opening of vinyl. Glue edge of

opening to shirt. Allow to dry.
5. Use pattern and appliqué fabric and follow Steps 2 and 3 of Making Appliqués, page 124.
6. Match edges of appliqué to drawn lines on shirt. Being careful not to touch vinyl with hot iron or to catch beads under appliqué, fuse appliqué to shirt.
7. For porthole hinge, refer to photo to draw a 1½" long line at right side of design. Being careful not to catch beads in stitching, follow Machine Appliquéing, page 125, to stitch over edges of appliqué and drawn line. Glue silver buttons to top and bottom of stitched line.
8. For porthole latch, refer to photo to glue hook portion of buckle to left side of porthole. Use metallic thread and Satin Stitch, page 127, to stitch over bar of buckle.
9. To launder, hand wash and hang to dry. Do not put in dryer.
10. For sunglasses, use cement to glue desired decorative items to frames.

PRAIRIE POINTS SKIRT   (Shown on page 45)

You will need a skirt (we used a denim skirt with slant pockets), coordinating bandanas, thread to match skirt, and embroidery floss to coordinate with bandanas.

1. Wash, dry, and press skirt and bandanas.
2. To determine number of prairie points needed, measure circumference of skirt hem and divide by 2. Cut determined number of 4″ squares from bandanas.
3. For prairie point edging, fold 1 square in half from top to bottom. Fold side edges to meet long raw edge, forming a triangle (Fig. 1); press. Repeat for remaining bandana squares.

Fig. 1

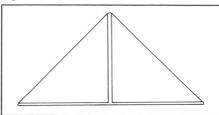

4. With right sides of triangles facing wrong side of skirt, refer to Fig. 2 to overlap and pin raw edges of triangles ¾″ above bottom edge of skirt. Whipstitch raw edges of triangles to skirt hem.

Fig. 2

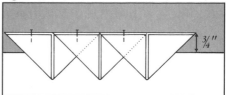

5. For pocket trim, refer to photo and use 3 strands of floss to work Fern Stitch, page 128, along edges of skirt pockets.

BANDANA SHIRT   (Shown on page 45)

You will need a shirt (we used a long-sleeved, button-front chambray shirt), coordinating bandanas with paisley motif, paper-backed fusible web, coordinating embroidery floss, embroidery hoop, and thread to match fabrics.

1. Wash, dry, and press shirt and bandanas.
2. (*Note:* Refer to photo for Steps 2 - 10.) For paisley cutouts, follow manufacturer's instructions to fuse web to wrong side of 1 bandana. Cut paisley motifs from bandana. Arrange cutouts on shirt. Follow manufacturer's instructions to fuse cutouts to shirt.
3. Use 2 strands of floss to work Fern Stitch, page 128, along raw edge of each cutout.
4. For shirt front binding, measure shirt front opening from bottom of collar band to hem; add ½″ to measurement.

Cut one 1½″ wide bias strip of bandana the determined measurement (pieced as necessary).

5. Press ends of strip ¼″ to wrong side. Match wrong sides and fold strip in half lengthwise; press. Fold long raw edges to center; press.
6. Unfold 1 long edge of binding. With right sides facing and matching unfolded edge of binding to edge of buttonhole side of shirt front opening, pin binding to shirt. Using pressed line as a guide, sew binding to shirt (Fig. 1).

Fig. 1

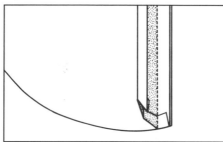

7. Fold binding over edge of shirt to wrong side; whipstitch in place.
8. For binding on cuffs, measure edge of 1 cuff and repeat Steps 4 - 7 for each cuff.
9. For collar trim, measure edge of collar; add ½″ to measurement. Cut one 2″ wide bias strip the determined measurement. Press ends of binding ¼″ to wrong side. Match wrong sides and fold strip in half lengthwise; press.
10. With folded edge of trim extending ⅜″ beyond edge of collar, pin trim to wrong side of collar. Whipstitch raw edges of trim in place; press.

You will need a men's shirt (we used a striped baseball uniform with button front), one 12″ x 15″ piece each of red and blue polyester satin, one 5″ square of white broadcloth, one 5″ square of fusible craft batting, lightweight fusible interfacing, paper-backed fusible web, thread to match fabrics, red embroidery floss, metallic gold middy braid, snaps (optional), washable fabric glue, tracing paper, item(s) to transfer pattern to fabric (see Transferring Patterns, page 124), see-through pressing cloth, and rip-away backing or medium weight paper.

1. Wash, dry, and press shirt, fabrics, and braid.

2. Referring to photo, glue braid to shirt front and around neckline; allow to dry.

3. Trace each large pattern (shown in blue), each small pattern (shown in red), and baseball pattern, this page and page 63, onto separate pieces of tracing paper; cut out.

4. Using blue satin for large patterns, red satin for small patterns, and white broadcloth for baseball pattern, follow Steps 2 - 4 of Making Appliqués, page 124; do not remove paper backing from blue satin appliqués.

5. Referring to patterns for placement, fuse red satin appliqués to blue satin appliqués.

6. For baseball appliqué, fuse baseball to right side of batting square; trim batting even with appliqué. Referring to photo, use white thread to sew along curved lines of laces. Use 2 strands of floss and straight stitches to sew along laces.

7. (*Note:* Buttons or buttonholes may be covered by appliqués. Remove buttons before fusing appliqués in place; replace with snaps after project is completed.) Remove paper backing from appliqués. Referring to Fig. 1, place appliqué on left shirt front with dotted lines even with opening of shirt; fuse appliqué in place except for fabric extending beyond shirt opening. Fold extending fabric to wrong side of shirt; fuse in place. Button shirt. Referring to photo, arrange remaining appliqués on right shirt front, making sure satin appliqués line up with appliqués on left shirt front; fuse in place.

Fig. 1

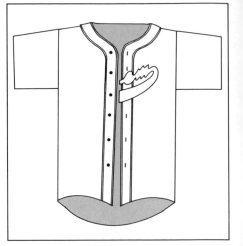

8. Follow Machine Appliquéing, page 125, to appliqué all raw edges.

9. To launder garment, follow glue manufacturer's recommendations.

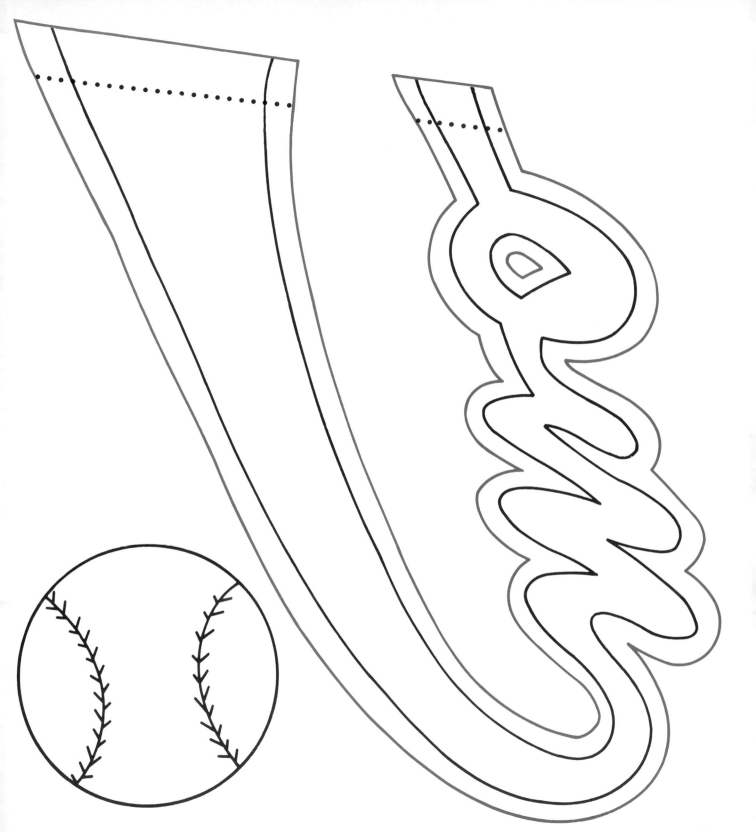

Fall

Fall rustles in with crisp, refreshing breezes to paint the days with reds and golds. Children head back to the classroom clad in their new school clothes, and we begin to plan our own wardrobes for the cool weather ahead. Warm sweaters and sweatshirts are perfect for the brisk days, and light jackets are nice for windy afternoons. Halloween is just around the corner, so it's time to prepare for spooky fun with costumes for the family, too! Our ideas for autumn clothes will help you enjoy every minute of this richly beautiful season.

Scarecrow Costume, page 85

''Ghost Crossing'' Tee, page 84
''Spooky Dad'' Sweatshirt, page 80
Clown Costume, page 91
Fairy Princess Costume, page 86

The entire family will have a ghoulishly good time on Halloween with these spooky clothes! For Mom, a painted tee features a ghostly trio, and Dad's appliquéd shirt is monstrously funny. Perfect for a little boy, the clown costume is created with a man's shirt, vest, and Bermuda shorts. A tulle skirt and iridescent accents make a plain pink leotard fit for a fairy princess.

Baby can join in the fun clad in a painted jack-o'-lantern shirt, and our creepy collection of footwear includes designs to please everyone.

Little Jack-O'-Lantern Shirt, page 83
Halloween Shoes, page 81

The rich hues of autumn look especially lovely on these tops. Colorful pansies make a spectacular showing on a sweatshirt — the vibrant blossoms are cut from dyed fabric and machine quilted for a three-dimensional effect. Cross-stitched leaves in rusts and golds add beauty to a brown sweater.

Pansy Sweatshirt, page 92

Autumn Leaves Sweater, page 79

Apple Jumper, page 87

Denim and plaid are a winning combination for back-to-school fashions! Overalls are transformed into a cute jumper by adding a demure skirt to the bib. The pockets are appliquéd with apples and sewn to the skirt. For a fun, flirty look, ruffles are added to cut-off blue jeans to create a short skirt. A denim jacket and backpack are dressed up to match with ruffles and bows. Painted wooden pins complete the outfit.

School Days Denim, page 76
School Scatter Pins, page 78

*T*hese grown-up styles will be right at home in the classroom — or anywhere! The quilt-block pockets on the sweatshirt cardigan feature an old-fashioned schoolhouse pattern; prairie point edging adds interest to the front opening. The attractive border on the coordinating skirt, shown on the opposite page, repeats the schoolhouse motif.

Chalkboard Sweatshirt, page 77
Patchwork Cardigan, page 88

*P*erfect for a mom or teacher, this smart appliquéd top has vinyl pockets to display treasured school pictures.

Patchwork Skirt, page 88

Menswear takes on a bold feminine look with these unique outfits. And since everything can be found in a thrift shop — or even your own attic — they're inexpensive, too. The crazy quilt pattern on this vest was created with old neckties, ribbon, and lace.

Adorned with vintage jewelry and buttons, clothing labels, and little bow ties, an old-fashioned lunch box becomes an unusual purse.

This sophisticated city shorts ensemble is made from a man's suit! It's accented with costume jewelry, buttons, clothing labels, and neckties. A man's fedora is embellished with a hatband made from another necktie to provide the perfect finishing touch.

Thrift Shop Treasures, page 82

For jacket, you will need a jean jacket, plaid ribbon same width as jacket cuffs, paper-backed fusible web, tracing paper, washable fabric glue, liquid fray preventative, craft knife, purchased double-fold bias tape, and thread to match bias tape.

For skirt, you will need a pair of jeans.

For backpack, you will need a backpack, purchased double-fold bias tape, thread to match bias tape, and washable fabric glue.

You will also need coordinating plaid fabrics, $\frac{7}{8}$"w plaid ribbon, thread to match fabrics and ribbon, and desired School Scatter Pins (page 78).

JACKET

1. (*Note:* Follow Steps 1 - 3 for each fabric inset.) For fabric inset pattern, refer to photo and place tracing paper over area of jacket to be covered with fabric; use a pencil to draw around area. Cut out pattern.

2. Cut a piece of fabric approximately 1" larger on all sides than pattern. Follow manufacturer's instructions to fuse web to wrong side of fabric piece. Use pattern and cut out fabric piece. Remove paper backing.

3. Place fabric web side down on jacket. Trim fabric to fit if necessary or use point of scissors to push raw edges of fabric under jacket seams. If area to be covered has a button on it, cut a slit in fabric over button and slip button through slit. Fuse fabric piece in place.

4. For ruffle at jacket opening, measure length of jacket opening and add $\frac{1}{2}$". Cut a length of bias tape the determined measurement. Cut a bias strip of fabric $4\frac{1}{2}$" wide and twice as long as the determined measurement.

5. Unfold ends of bias tape; press ends $\frac{1}{4}$" to wrong side. With wrong sides together, press fabric strip in half lengthwise. Baste $\frac{3}{8}$" and $\frac{1}{4}$" from long raw edge. Pull basting threads, gathering ruffle to same length as bias tape. Referring to Fig. 1, fold each short edge of ruffle to 1 side (wrong side) to meet long raw edge of ruffle; baste in place. Insert raw edge of ruffle between folded edges of bias tape. Stitch ruffle and bias tape together close to inner edge of bias tape.

Fig. 1

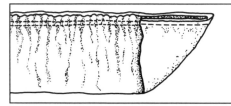

6. Referring to photo, glue ruffle to inside edge of jacket opening; allow to dry.

7. For each cuff, measure 1 long edge of cuff; add 1". Cut a length of ribbon (same width as cuff) the determined measurement. Press ends of ribbon $\frac{1}{2}$" to 1 side (wrong side); glue to secure. Glue ribbon to inside of cuff; allow to dry. Use craft knife to cut a slit through ribbon at jacket buttonhole. Apply fray preventative to cut edges; allow to dry.

8. For each bow, cut one $6\frac{1}{2}$" x 13" piece of fabric. With wrong side out, overlap short edges of fabric 1" to form a loop; use a $\frac{1}{4}$" seam allowance and sew along each raw edge where indicated by dashed lines in Fig. 2. Cut corners diagonally and turn right side out through overlapped area (back of bow).

Fig. 2

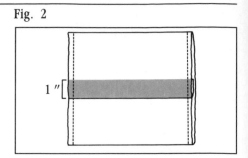

1 "

9. For center of each bow, cut one $3\frac{1}{2}$" length of $\frac{7}{8}$" wide ribbon. Fanfold bow; wrap ribbon around center, overlapping ends at back. Whipstitch ends of ribbon in place.

10. Tack bows to jacket. Attach School Scatter Pins to jacket.

11. To launder, remove pins and follow glue manufacturer's recommendations.

SKIRT

1. For skirt yoke, cut off jeans 2" below bottom of zipper placket, being careful not to cut back pockets. If jeans have front pocket linings, trim linings even with raw edge of yoke. Baste linings and yoke together close to raw edges. To finish raw edge of yoke, use a medium zigzag stitch with a medium stitch length to stitch over raw edge.

2. For double ruffle, measure circumference of bottom of yoke; multiply by 2. Cut one 5" wide and one 8" wide fabric strip the determined measurement.

3. With right sides facing and matching short edges, fold 5" wide fabric strip in half. Use a $\frac{1}{2}$" seam allowance and sew short edges together to form a loop. Press seam open. Press 1 raw edge $\frac{1}{4}$" to wrong side; press $\frac{1}{4}$" to wrong side again and stitch in place. Turn right side out. Repeat for 8" wide fabric strip.

SCHOOL DAYS DENIM (continued)

4. Matching raw edges, insert 8" wide loop in 5" wide loop. Baste loops together ⅜" and ¼" from raw edge (top edge). Pull basting threads, drawing up gathers to fit bottom of yoke. With wrong side of ruffle facing right side of yoke, overlap ruffle over yoke with top edge of ruffle 1½" above bottom edge of yoke. Baste in place.

5. For bias trim, measure circumference of skirt yoke at top of ruffle; add 1". Cut one 1¼" wide bias strip of fabric the determined measurement. Press long edges and 1 short edge of strip ¼" to wrong side. Beginning with raw edge of strip at 1 side seam, center bias strip over raw edge of ruffle. Baste in place. Stitching close to each long edge, stitch strip to skirt. Remove any visible basting threads.

6. For bow, follow Steps 8 and 9 of Jacket instructions, page 76. Tack bow to bias trim.

7. Attach School Scatter Pins to skirt. Remove pins before laundering.

BACKPACK

1. For ruffle, measure along edge of backpack flap and add ½"; follow Steps 4 - 6 of Jacket instructions, page 76.

2. For bow, follow Steps 8 and 9 of Jacket instructions, page 76. Tack bow to backpack flap.

3. Attach School Scatter Pins to backpack.

4. To launder, remove pins and follow glue manufacturer's recommendations.

CHALKBOARD SWEATSHIRT (Shown on page 72)

You will need a sweatshirt; red, green, brown, and black fabrics for appliqués; thread to coordinate with fabrics; lightweight fusible interfacing; paper-backed fusible web; tracing paper; rip-away backing or medium weight paper; one 5" square of clear lightweight vinyl for each photo pocket (available at fabric stores); white Pentel® Fabricfun™ Pastel Dye Stick (available in sets at craft or art supply stores); removable fabric marking pen; see-through pressing cloth; and desired wallet size photo(s).

1. For apple, leaf, and stem patterns, follow Tracing Patterns, page 124. For chalkboard pattern, draw an 8¼" x 5¾" rectangle on tracing paper. For chalkboard border pattern, draw a 9½" x 7" rectangle on tracing paper. Cut out patterns.

2. To appliqué shirt, follow Making Appliqués, page 124, and Machine Appliquéing, page 125.

3. Use dye stick to write "school days" on chalkboard appliqué. Follow manufacturer's instructions to heat-set words.

4. For photo pocket pattern, draw a 2¼" x 3" rectangle on tracing paper; cut out.

5. For each photo pocket, center pattern on 1 apple; use fabric marking pen to draw around pattern. Center vinyl over drawn rectangle on apple. Using a straight stitch and stitching along side and bottom lines of drawn rectangle, sew vinyl to shirt. Trim vinyl ⅛" from stitching lines; trim vinyl even with top drawn line. Remove any visible pen lines. Insert 1 photo in each pocket.

6. To launder, remove photos and hand wash in cool water; hang to dry. Do not put in dryer.

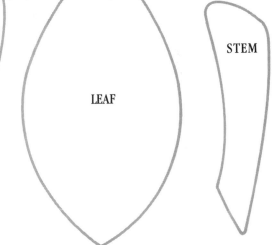

APPLE

LEAF

STEM

For heart pin, you will need one 2¼"w wooden heart cutout.

For large or small apple pin, you will need a 1"w or a 3"w wooden apple cutout.

For ruler pin, you will need one 6" long jumbo craft stick.

For bear pin, you will need a 3" h wooden bear cutout, graphite transfer paper, and tracing paper.

For pencil pin, you will need one 6" long jumbo craft stick, graphite transfer paper, and tracing paper.

For slate pin, you will need a 2" x 3" miniature slate (available at craft stores), desired acrylic paint, and ¾"h wooden letter cutouts.

You will also need acrylic paint (see color key), black permanent felt-tip pen with fine point (except for slate pin or apple pins), paintbrushes, matte clear acrylic spray, 1" long pin back, hot glue gun, and glue sticks.

Note: Refer to photo when painting pin. Allow paint to dry between colors.

1. Apply 1 coat of acrylic spray to wooden cutout or craft stick. Allow to dry.

2. For heart pin or large or small apple pin, refer to color key to paint cutout.

3. For ruler pin, trim ⅜" from each end of craft stick. Refer to color key to paint stick.

4. For bear pin or pencil pin, trace desired portion of pattern onto tracing paper. Use transfer paper to transfer pattern to cutout or craft stick. Use scissors to trim craft stick along pencil point. Refer to color key to paint cutout or craft stick.

5. For slate pin, paint letter cutouts desired colors. Glue letters to slate; allow to dry.

6. Allowing to dry between coats, spray pin with 2 coats of acrylic spray.

7. Glue pin back to back of pin.

HEART
Heart - red
Plaid design - black pen and yellow, green, and blue

APPLES
Apple - red shaded with dk grey and highlighted with white
Leaves - green

RULER
Ruler - yellow
Top edge - black
Markings and numbers - black pen

PENCIL
Pencil - yellow
Eraser - red
Bands below eraser - gold
Pencil point and detail lines - black pen

BEAR
Body - brown
Vest - blue
Collar and buttons - green
Pants - blue and green
Paws, cheeks, and ears - lt pink
Face and outlines - black pen

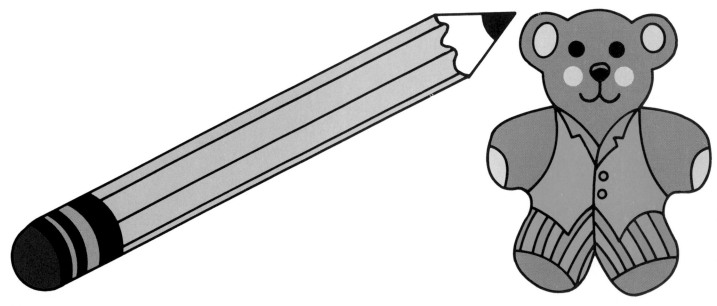

AUTUMN LEAVES SWEATER (Shown on page 69)

You will need a sweater, a 13″ x 14″ piece of 10 mesh waste canvas, masking tape, medium weight non-fusible interfacing, sewing thread, embroidery floss (see color key), embroidery hoop (optional), tweezers, and a spray bottle filled with water.

Referring to photo, follow Working On Waste Canvas, page 127, to stitch design on sweater. Use 5 strands of floss for Cross Stitch and 2 for Backstitch.

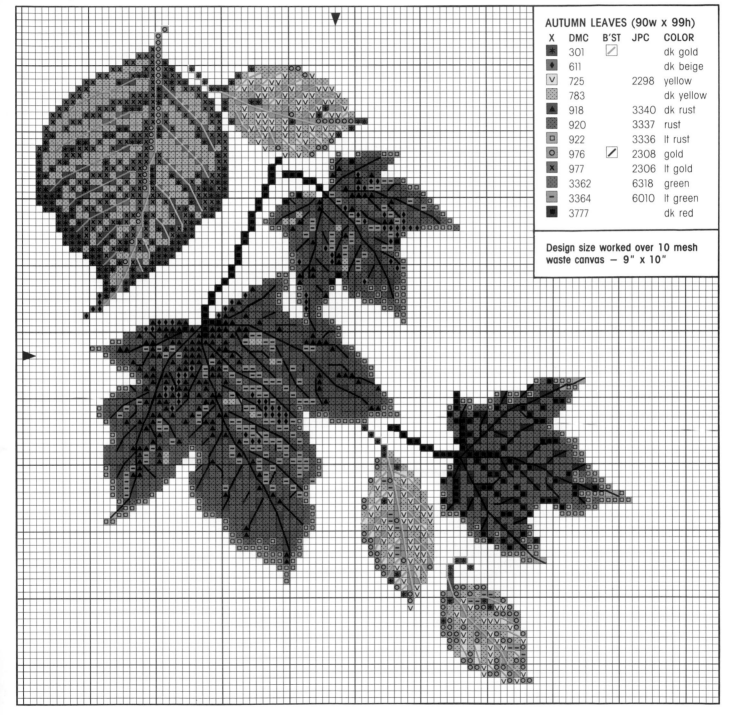

AUTUMN LEAVES (90w x 99h)

X	DMC	B'ST	JPC	COLOR
✳	301	╱		dk gold
◆	611			dk beige
V	725		2298	yellow
░	783			dk yellow
▲	918		3340	dk rust
▨	920		3337	rust
▫	922		3336	lt rust
O	976	╱	2308	gold
X	977		2306	lt gold
▓	3362		6318	green
−	3364		6010	lt green
◼	3777			dk red

Design size worked over 10 mesh waste canvas — 9″ x 10″

"SPOOKY DAD" SWEATSHIRT (Shown on page 66)

You will need a sweatshirt, fabrics for appliqués, dimensional fabric paints in squeeze bottles to coordinate with fabrics, lightweight fusible interfacing, paper-backed fusible web, item(s) to transfer pattern to fabric (see Transferring Patterns, page 124), removable fabric marking pen, see-through pressing cloth, T-shirt form or cardboard covered with waxed paper, and tracing paper.

1. Use patterns and follow Tracing Patterns, page 124. Cut out patterns.
2. (*Note:* Refer to photo for Steps 2 - 4.) Follow Making Appliqués, page 124, to make mouth appliqué and letter appliqués to spell "SPOOKY DAD."
3. Use fabric marking pen to draw zigzag lines above each "O."
4. Follow Steps 2 - 7 of Dimensional Fabric Painting, page 125, to apply paint to appliqués and drawn lines.

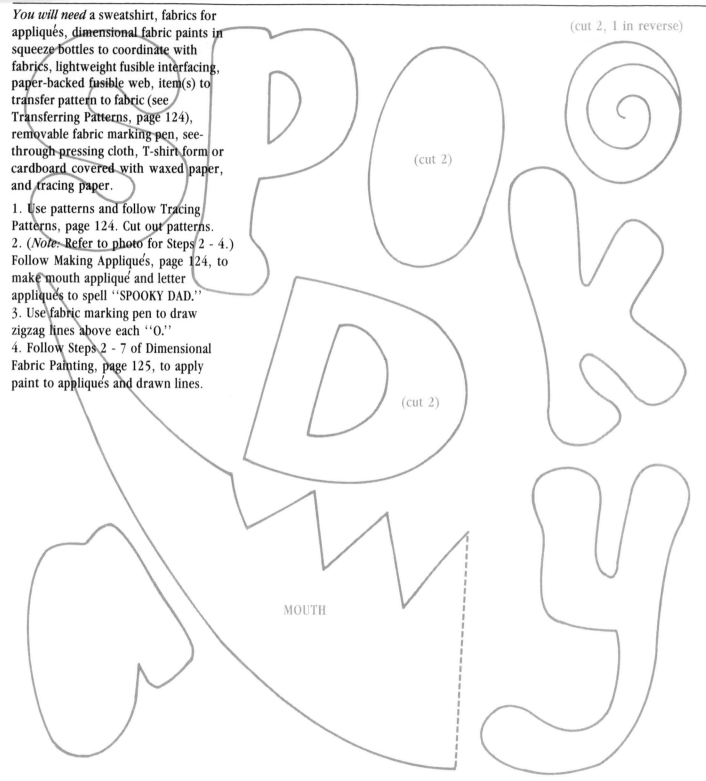

(cut 2, 1 in reverse)

(cut 2)

(cut 2)

MOUTH

80

HALLOWEEN SHOES (Shown on page 67)

SPIDER SHOES

You will need a pair of shoes (we used infants' oxford-style shoes); black, white, and orange acrylic paint; yellow and black $\frac{1}{16}$"w satin ribbon for laces; and paintbrushes.

1. Remove laces from shoes.
2. (*Note:* Refer to photo when painting shoes. Allow to dry between colors.) Paint saddle portion of each shoe orange.
3. For each spider, paint a small black oval on toe of shoe. Paint 8 black legs extending from ends of oval. Paint 2 white dots for eyes. Paint black dots in centers of eyes. For web, paint a dotted line extending from spider to top of shoe.
4. Relace each shoe with 1 length each of yellow and black ribbon.

JACK-O'-LANTERN SHOES

You will need a pair of shoes (we used black canvas slip-on tennis shoes), orange and white fabric, lightweight fusible interfacing, paper-backed fusible web, item(s) to transfer patterns to fabric (see Transferring Patterns, page 124), see-through pressing cloth, $\frac{1}{2}$"w orange and yellow rickrack, black fabric paint, small round paintbrush, tracing paper, and washable fabric glue.

1. Use jack-o'-lantern and ghost patterns and follow Tracing Patterns; cut out patterns. Use patterns and follow Steps 2 - 5 of Making Appliqués, page 124.
2. Paint ghost eyes and jack-o'-lantern faces; allow to dry. Follow manufacturer's instructions to heat-set paint if necessary.
3. Measure area on 1 shoe to be trimmed with rickrack; add 2". Cut 1 piece from each color rickrack the determined measurement. Referring to photo, twist rickrack pieces together. Glue to shoe, trimming to fit. Repeat for remaining shoe.

"BOO" SHOES

You will need a pair of shoes (we used children's black suede lace-up tennis shoes), white fabric paint, small round paintbrush, item(s) to transfer pattern to shoes (see Transferring Patterns, page 124), tracing paper, $\frac{1}{4}$"w orange grosgrain ribbon for laces, four $\frac{3}{8}$" dia. black beads, and craft glue.

1. Trace "BOO" pattern onto tracing paper. Follow Transferring Patterns, page 124, to transfer design to each shoe.
2. Referring to photo, paint design; allow to dry. Follow manufacturer's instructions to heat-set paint if necessary.
3. Remove laces from shoes. Relace each shoe with 1 length of ribbon.
4. Thread 1 bead onto 1 ribbon end, leaving 1" of ribbon exposed. Dip $\frac{1}{4}$" of end of ribbon in glue. Pull bead down over glued area; allow to dry. Repeat for remaining ribbon ends.

BAT SHOES

You will need a pair of shoes (we used orange lace-up tennis shoes), black and yellow fabric paint, small round paintbrushes, item(s) to transfer pattern to shoes (see Transferring Patterns, page 124), tracing paper, and 1"w ribbon for laces.

Use bat and city pattern and follow Steps 1 - 3 of "BOO" Shoes instructions, reversing pattern for left shoe.

Many of the items used in the following projects such as clothing, neckties, buttons, and jewelry may be found in thrift stores, resale shops, and flea markets.

SUIT

You will need a men's suit, neckties, buttons, jewelry, labels cut from clothing, 1"w single-fold bias tape to match suit, ¾"w elastic, and thread to match suit and neckties.

1. (*Note*: Refer to photo for Steps 1 - 6.) For each small bow tie, cut one 9" length from narrow end of 1 necktie. Overlap ends 1" to form a loop; tack ends in place.
2. For center of tie, cut one 1" x 2" strip of fabric from a contrasting necktie. Press long edges ¼" to wrong side. Wrap strip tightly around center of loop; tack overlapped ends of strip in place at back of bow.
3. For each small necktie, tie a knot approximately 4" from narrow end of 1 necktie. Cut necktie even with top of knot.
4. For breast pocket, cut narrow end of 1 necktie 2" longer than breast pocket opening; press raw edge 1" to wrong side. Pin necktie in place. Arrange jewelry over necktie. Hand stitch necktie and jewelry in place.
5. For each pocket flap, cut narrow end of 1 necktie same length as flap. With point of necktie 1" to 2" from 1 short edge of flap, place necktie along bottom edge of flap; fold raw edge of necktie to wrong side of flap. Hand stitch necktie in place. Cut a 1" wide strip of necktie fabric 2" longer than flap; press long edges ¼" to wrong side. Matching 1 long edge of strip to top edge of flap, center strip on flap; fold ends of strip to wrong side of flap. Hand stitch in place.

6. Arrange small bow ties, small neckties, buttons, and labels on jacket; securely tack in place.
7. To cinch back of jacket at waist, try on jacket and mark waistline with pin at center back of jacket. Cut one 14" length of bias tape for casing; press ends ½" to wrong side. Center bias tape over pin mark on inside of jacket and stitch long edges of tape in place. Cut one 10" length of elastic. Thread elastic through casing; securely whipstitch ends of elastic to ends of casing.
8. For shorts, cut off legs of pants 3½" longer than desired finished length. Press each raw edge ½" to wrong side; press 2" to wrong side again and hem. Press bottom edge of hem 1" to right side to form cuff; tack in place.
9. Suit must be dry-cleaned.

VEST

You will need a men's suit vest; neckties; buttons; lace, gimp and metallic gold trims; labels cut from clothing; ribbon; coordinating embroidery floss; dry-cleanable paper-backed fusible web; aluminum foil; thread to match vest, neckties, and trims; seam ripper; and see-through pressing cloth.

1. Use seam ripper to remove vest and lining seams at shoulders and sides. Set vest back aside. Baste raw edges of lining and vest front together. Remove buttons; press.
2. To prepare neckties for fusing, remove center back seam from each necktie; trim away lining and press. Follow manufacturer's instructions to fuse web to wrong sides of neckties. Remove paper backing.
3. To prepare ribbon and clothing labels for fusing, cut ribbon into

approximately 12" lengths. Place a sheet of aluminum foil shiny side up on ironing board. Place ribbon lengths and labels right sides down on foil. Place a sheet of web over ribbon lengths and labels; follow manufacturer's instructions to fuse web to ribbons and labels. Allow to cool. Remove paper backing. Peel ribbon lengths and labels from foil; trim excess web.
4. (*Note:* Follow Steps 4 - 9 for each side of vest front.) Place 1 side of vest front right side up on ironing board. Cut web-backed neckties into desired shapes. Referring to photo and overlapping edges, arrange pieces on vest front. Fuse in place.
5. To cover raw edges of necktie pieces (except along edges of vest front), refer to photo and use the following:

   Web-backed ribbon - cut desired lengths; fuse in place.
   Lace or other trims - cut desired lengths; hand stitch in place.
   Fern Stitch (page 128) - use 3 strands of floss.
   Necktie fabric pieces without web - cut strips from necktie pieces; press edges to wrong side. Hand stitch in place.

6. For armhole binding, measure edge of armhole. Cut one 2" wide bias strip from 1 necktie (without web) the determined measurement (pieced as necessary). With wrong sides together, fold strip in half lengthwise and press; fold long raw edges to center and press again.
7. Unfold 1 long edge of binding. With right sides together and matching unfolded edge of binding to armhole edge, pin binding to vest. Using a ½" seam allowance, sew binding to vest. Fold binding over raw edge to back of vest; whipstitch in place.

8. Using a single binding strip, repeat Steps 6 and 7 to bind front and bottom edge.

9. Referring to photo, fuse labels to vest front; sew buttons to vest front.

10. To reassemble vest, match raw edges and place vest front pieces and vest back right sides together. Using approximately the same seam allowance as originally used, sew shoulder seams and side seams. To finish seams, use a medium zigzag stitch with a medium stitch length to stitch over raw edges of seams; press.

11. Vest must be dry-cleaned.

HATS

For each hat, you will need a hat, 1 or more neckties, and thread to match necktie(s).

1. For hatband, refer to photo, page 75, and tie necktie around crown of hat. Trim narrow end of tie 2″ from knot. Tuck cut end of necktie under hatband and tack in place.

2. (*Note:* If necktie roses are desired, follow Steps 2 - 4 for each rose.) Cut 18″ from narrow end of 1 necktie. Baste along 1 long edge of necktie length. Pull basting thread, gathering necktie to 12″.

3. Beginning with raw edge, loosely roll up necktie. For base of rose, pinch gathered edge of necktie together; pulling stitches tight, make several stitches through pinched area to secure.

4. Tack rose to hatband.

PURSE

You will need a metal lunch box, neckties, thread to match neckties, buttons, jewelry, pieces of trim, keys, labels cut from clothing, desired color acrylic paint, foam brush, matte clear acrylic spray, and household cement.

1. Paint lunch box; allow to dry. Apply 2 coats of acrylic spray to lunch box, allowing to dry between coats.

2. For each small bow tie, follow Steps 1 and 2 of Suit instructions, page 82.

3. For each extra-small bow tie, cut one 6″ piece from narrow end of 1 necktie and repeat Step 2. For each large bow tie, cut one 10″ piece from narrow end of 1 necktie and repeat Step 2.

4. Referring to photo, glue bow ties, buttons, jewelry, trims, keys, and labels to lunch box.

LITTLE JACK-O'-LANTERN SHIRT (Shown on page 67)

You will need a T-shirt, fabric paint (see color key), paintbrushes, black and green permanent felt-tip pens with fine points, item(s) to transfer patterns to shirt (see Transferring Patterns, page 124), and tracing paper.

1. Wash, dry, and press shirt according to paint manufacturer's recommendations.

2. Trace patterns onto tracing paper.

3. (*Note:* Refer to photo for Steps 3 - 5.) Follow Transferring Patterns, page 124, to transfer patterns to shirt.

4. Allowing to dry between colors, refer to color key to paint shirt.

5. For tendrils, use black and green pens to draw wavy lines around leaves. Use silver glitter paint to paint several sets of 3 dots among tendrils.

6. If necessary, heat-set design according to paint manufacturer's recommendations.

7. To launder, follow paint manufacturer's recommendations.

COLOR KEY
Pumpkin - orange with white highlights
Pumpkin eyes, nose, and mouth - yellow
Pupils - black with white highlights
Stem and leaves - green with yellow and white highlights
Bat - black with silver glitter eyes
Spider and web - black
Spider eyes - white with silver glitter highlights
Outlines and detail lines - black
Grass (paint freehand) - green, yellow, and black

"GHOST CROSSING" TEE (Shown on page 66)

You will need a T-shirt (we used a long-sleeved T-shirt); orange, black, brown, lt brown, green, and dk green fabric paint; white dimensional fabric paint in squeeze bottle; iridescent glitter; paintbrushes; tracing paper; item(s) to transfer patterns to shirt (see Transferring Patterns, page 124); and T-shirt form or cardboard covered with waxed paper.

1. Wash, dry, and press shirt according to paint manufacturers' recommendations.
2. (*Note*: Refer to photo for Steps 2 - 4.) Trace signpost and ghost patterns, this page and page 85, onto tracing paper. Follow Transferring Patterns, page 124, to transfer patterns to shirt. Insert T-shirt form into shirt.
3. (*Note:* Allow paint to dry between colors.) Referring to color key, paint design.
4. To outline each ghost with dimensional paint, follow Steps 3 - 5 of Dimensional Fabric Painting, page 125. While paint is still wet, sprinkle glitter over paint, coating well. Allow paint to dry. Shake off excess glitter.
5. To launder, follow paint manufacturers' recommendations.

COLOR KEY
Ghosts - white dimensional paint
    (brushed on)
Ghosts' eyes - black
Signpost - lt brown shaded with brown
Sign - green shaded with dk green
Letters and detail lines on sign and
    signpost - black
Jack-o'-lantern - orange
Jack-o'-lantern face, detail lines,
    shading, and handle - black
Grass (paint freehand) - green

SCARECROW COSTUME (Shown on page 65)

You will need men's overalls and a flannel shirt (we found ours at a thrift store), bandana, thread to match overalls and bandana, gardening gloves, straw plant basket for hat, natural-colored raffia, ⅜"w grosgrain ribbon to match raffia, rope for belt, 2 artificial blackbirds with wired feet, scrap fabrics for patches, paper-backed fusible web, black permanent felt-tip pen with fine point, and craft glue.

1. For cuffs, cut off legs of overalls 4" longer than desired length. Fold raw edge of each leg 2" to right side; fold 2" to right side again. Tack in place.
2. For patches on overalls, cut desired size squares from fabrics. Follow manufacturer's instructions to fuse web to wrong sides of squares. Referring to photo for placement, fuse patches to overalls. Use black pen to draw lines resembling stitches along edges of each patch.
3. Cut raffia into approximately 10" lengths.
4. For wrist cuffs, measure around child's wrist; add 20". Cut 4 lengths of ribbon the determined measurement.

5. Center a line of glue the length of the child's wrist measurement on 1 ribbon length. Referring to Fig. 1, spread raffia evenly over glued area. Apply glue evenly over 1 side of a second ribbon length. Matching edges of ribbons, place second ribbon on top of raffia, glue side down. Allow to dry. Referring to Fig. 2, trim raffia even with 1 long edge (top) of ribbon; trim remaining raffia approximately 8" from ribbon. Repeat for remaining cuff.

Fig. 1

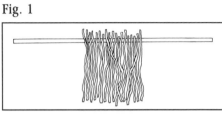

Fig. 2

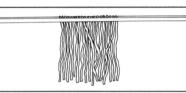

6. For ankle cuffs, measure around child's ankle and repeat Steps 4 and 5.

7. For bandana, cut two 16" lengths of ribbon. Apply glue evenly to 1 side of 1 ribbon length. Repeat Step 5, spreading raffia evenly over entire ribbon length.
8. With right sides together, press bandana in half diagonally; unfold bandana. Center raffia strip on bandana with top edge of ribbon matching pressed line. Refold bandana along pressed line. Stitching through all layers, sew bandana and raffia strip together ½" from pressed edge. Turn right side out. With wrong sides together, press bandana in half diagonally. Trim raffia to 3" above bandana.
9. For hat, cut edge from rim of plant basket; fringe edges of basket 2".
10. Refer to photo to wire birds to hat.
11. For rope belt, measure around child's waist; add 20". Cut a length of rope the determined measurement. Knot rope 2" from each end.
12. Place lengths of raffia in bib pocket of overalls.
13. Refer to photo to assemble costume.

SKIRT

You will need two 36"w strips 7 yds long of white tulle for skirt, 17"w iridescent patterned netting for belt (see Step 8 for amount), purchased 1"w white quilt binding, ½"w elastic, 20" of ⅜"w pink grosgrain ribbon, iridescent glitter dimensional fabric paint in squeeze bottle, ¾" dia. white iridescent paillettes (large round sequins with holes), 1/16"w pink satin ribbon, washable jewel glue, white thread, and heavy thread (buttonhole twist).

1. For skirt, measure around child's waist; multiply by 2. For waistband, cut 1 length of quilt binding the determined measurement. Press ends of binding ½" to wrong side.

2. To gather skirt, place tulle pieces together. Place heavy thread on tulle ½" from 1 long edge; zigzag over heavy thread, being careful not to stitch into thread. Pull heavy thread, gathering tulle to fit binding. Insert gathered edge between long folded edges of binding. Stitch through all layers close to inner edge of binding.

3. Place skirt on a protected flat surface. Referring to photo, paint long vertical lines on skirt. Allow to dry.

4. For each paillette, cut a 5" length of 1/16" wide ribbon. Thread ribbon through paillette and tie into a bow. Glue bow to skirt. Allow to dry.

5. Add 1" to child's waist measurement; cut elastic the determined measurement. Thread elastic through binding. Overlapping ends of elastic 1", sew ends together.

6. Try skirt on child. If necessary, trim skirt to desired length.

7. For belt loops, cut four 5" lengths of ⅜" wide ribbon. Overlapping ends ½", sew ends of each length together to form a loop. Spacing loops evenly around waistband, tack loops to waistband.

8. Add 2 yards to child's waist measurement; cut a length of patterned netting the determined measurement. Thread netting through belt loops. Tie into a bow at back of skirt.

TOP

You will need pink leotard and footless tights, white tulle (see Steps 5 and 6 for amounts), iridescent glitter and pearl dimensional fabric paint in squeeze bottles, eight 5mm and nineteen 7mm crystal rhinestone jewels, ¾" dia. white iridescent paillettes (large round sequins with holes), 1/16"w pink satin ribbon, ⅜"w pink grosgrain ribbon for cuffs, tracing paper, item(s) to transfer pattern to leotard (see Transferring Patterns, page 124), white and pink thread, T-shirt form or cardboard covered with waxed paper, flat paintbrush, and washable jewel glue.

1. Wash, dry, and press leotard according to paint manufacturer's recommendations. Insert T-shirt form into leotard.

2. Referring to photo, use large pattern, this page, and follow Tracing Patterns and Transferring Patterns, page 124, to transfer pattern to leotard.

3. Use paintbrush and iridescent glitter paint to paint design; allow to dry. Use pearl paint and follow Steps 3 - 6 of Dimensional Fabric Painting, page 125, to paint over thick lines on design.

4. Glue large jewels over ■'s and small jewels over ✖'s. Allow to dry.

5. For each shoulder pouf, cut two 10" x 12" pieces of tulle. Place tulle pieces together. Use scissors to round off corners. Beginning at 1 long edge, baste across center of pieces. Pull basting threads, drawing up gathers to 2" wide; knot threads and trim ends. Match gathered line of pouf to center top of sleeve seam; securely tack in place. Finger press pouf toward sleeve.

6. For wrist ruffles, measure child's wrist; add 10". Cut 4 pieces of tulle 4" wide by the determined measurement. Add 20" to wrist measurement; cut 2 pieces of ⅜" wide ribbon the determined measurement.

7. For each ruffle, place 2 pieces of tulle together. Baste ¼" and ⅛" from 1 long edge. Pull basting threads, drawing up gathers to fit child's wrist.

8. Center gathered edge of tulle on 1 side of 1 ribbon; pin in place. Sewing close to each long edge of ribbon, stitch tulle to ribbon. Use scissors to round off corners of tulle.

9. Follow Steps 3 and 4 of Skirt instructions to apply paint and paillettes to shoulder poufs and wrist ruffles.

10. Use paintbrush to apply iridescent glitter paint to stitched area of each wrist ruffle ribbon; allow to dry. Center 1 large jewel on each ribbon; glue to secure. Allow to dry.

SLIPPERS

You will need ballet slippers, iridescent glitter and pearl dimensional fabric paint in squeeze bottles, eighteen 7mm crystal rhinestone jewels, item(s) to transfer pattern to slippers (see Transferring Patterns, page 124), flat paintbrush, tracing paper, and washable jewel glue.

1. Use small pattern, this page, and follow Tracing Patterns and Transferring Patterns, page 124, to transfer pattern to toe of each shoe.

2. Follow Step 3 of Top instructions to paint design on each shoe.

3. Glue jewels over ■'s; allow to dry.

FAIRY PRINCESS COSTUME (continued)

TIARA

You will need a plastic headband, ⅞"w metallic silver ribbon, white tulle, white thread, wired silver star garland, iridescent glitter dimensional fabric paint in squeeze bottle, hot glue gun, and glue sticks.

1. Overlapping edges, wrap ribbon around headband; glue to secure.
2. Cut two 7" x 8" pieces and one 8" x 12" piece of tulle.

3. Sewing through 1 layer of tulle, follow Step 5 of Top instructions, page 86, to gather each tulle piece. Refer to photo to glue gathered edges of tulle pieces to top of headband.
4. Follow Step 3 of Skirt instructions, page 86, to paint vertical lines on tulle pieces.
5. Cut desired lengths of garland. Wrap garland pieces around headband. Twist together to secure.

WAND

You will need a purchased silver wand with sequined star (we found ours at a craft store), metallic silver artificial grass, wired silver star garland, hot glue gun, and glue sticks.

Cut grass and garland desired lengths. Referring to photo, glue grass and garland to back of wand.

APPLE JUMPER   (Shown on page 70)

You will need a pair of overalls with back patch pockets, plaid fabric for skirt (see Step 4 for amount), plaid fabric for hem trim (see Step 6 for amount), two 5" squares of red print fabric for apple appliqués, four 3" squares of green print fabric for apple leaves, two 3½" x 24" bias strips of plaid fabric for waist ties, seam ripper, tracing paper, removable fabric marking pen, paper-backed fusible web, thread to match fabrics, lightweight fusible interfacing, and rip-away backing or medium weight paper.

1. Wash, dry, and press overalls and fabrics.
2. Use seam ripper to remove back pockets from overalls; set pockets aside.
3. For bib, follow Step 2 of Watermelon Jumper instructions, page 52.
4. For skirt, measure from waistline of bib to desired hemline. Measure bottom edge of bib front; multiply by 2½. Cut 2 skirt pieces the determined measurements.
5. Beginning 5" below top edge of skirt, follow Step 4 of Watermelon Jumper instructions, page 52, to sew skirt together.

6. (*Note*: Use a ¼" seam allowance for Steps 6 - 9.) For hem trim, measure bottom circumference of skirt; add ½". Cut a strip of fabric 7" wide by the determined measurement (piecing as necessary). Matching right sides and short edges, sew short edges of strip together to form a loop. Matching wrong sides and raw edges, press strip in half.
7. For hem, press bottom edge of skirt 1½" to wrong side. With folded edge of trim extending 2" beyond hem of skirt, insert trim into skirt. Stitch all layers together 1¼" above skirt hem.
8. Follow Steps 14 - 16 of Watermelon Jumper instructions, page 52, to attach bib to skirt.
9. Using bias strips and referring to Fig. 1, follow Steps 17 and 18 of Watermelon Jumper instructions, pages 52 and 53, to attach ties at waist.

Fig. 1

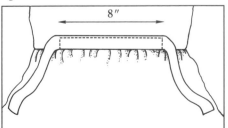

10. For appliqués on pockets, use apple and leaf patterns and follow Tracing Patterns, page 124. Cut out patterns.
11. Leaving bottom edges of leaves open, use leaf pattern and follow Sewing Shapes, page 124, to make 2 leaves; press. Baste ¼" from bottom edge of each leaf. Pull basting threads, gathering bottom of each leaf to ⅜".
12. (*Note:* Refer to photo for Steps 12 - 15.) Follow Steps 2 - 4 of Making Appliqués, page 124, to prepare 2 apple appliqués (1 in reverse).
13. For each apple, center appliqué on 1 back pocket. Place bottom edge of leaf ¼" under top edge of apple; pin leaf to pocket. Fuse apple in place.
14. Follow Machine Appliquéing, page 125, to appliqué apple to pocket.
15. Pin pockets to jumper. Check placement of pocket by trying jumper on, adjusting as necessary. Sew pockets to jumper along side and bottom edges.

For cardigan, you will need a sweatshirt; fabric for bias trim at neck, bottom edge, and front opening (see Step 3 for amounts); fabric for cuffs (see Step 11 for amount); fabric scraps for prairie point edging; and two $6\frac{1}{2}$" fabric squares for pocket linings.
For skirt, you will need a softly pleated or gathered skirt.
You will also need unbleached muslin and print fabrics for quilt blocks and sashing, thread to match fabrics, acetate sheets for templates (available at craft or art supply stores), permanent felt-tip pen with fine point, and fabric marking pencil.

CARDIGAN

1. Wash, dry, and press sweatshirt and fabrics.
2. For front opening of cardigan, use fabric marking pencil to draw a line at center front of shirt from neckband to waistband; cut along marked line. Cut off waistband of shirt. Cut sleeves to $\frac{1}{2}$" longer than desired finished length.
3. For bias trim at neck, measure around bottom edge of neckband; cut a bias strip of fabric 1" wide by the determined measurement. For bias trim at bottom edge, measure around bottom edge of shirt; cut a bias strip of fabric (pieced as necessary) 2" wide by the determined measurement. For bias trim at front opening, measure 1 raw edge at front opening and add 1". Cut 2 bias strips of fabric (pieced as necessary) $2\frac{1}{2}$" wide by the determined measurement.
4. Press long raw edges of 1" wide bias strip $\frac{1}{4}$" to wrong side. Press each remaining bias strip in half lengthwise with wrong sides together; press long

raw edges to center. Unfold ends of each $2\frac{1}{2}$" wide bias strip and press ends $\frac{1}{2}$" to wrong side. Refold ends.
5. For trim at neck, match 1 long edge (top edge) of trim to bottom edge of neckband and pin trim to shirt; blindstitch in place.
6. For trim at bottom edge of shirt, unfold 1 long edge of trim. With right side of trim facing wrong side of shirt and matching unfolded edge of trim to bottom raw edge of shirt, pin trim to shirt. Using a $\frac{1}{2}$" seam allowance, sew trim to shirt. Fold trim over raw edge to front of shirt; blindstitch in place.
7. For trim at left front opening, use a $\frac{5}{8}$" seam allowance and repeat Step 6 to sew 1 length of trim over left raw edge of front opening.
8. For prairie point edging, measure right raw edge of front opening and divide by 2. Cut the determined number of $2\frac{1}{2}$" squares from fabrics. Follow Step 3 of Prairie Points Skirt instructions, page 61, to make prairie points.
9. Matching wrong sides and raw edges and overlapping points, pin points along right raw edge of front opening; baste points in place.
10. Using a $\frac{5}{8}$" seam allowance, repeat Step 6 to sew remaining length of trim over right raw edge of front opening. Press trim to right side of shirt along blindstitched edge so prairie points extend past edge of opening; blindstitch trim in place.
11. For cuffs, measure circumference of 1 sleeve at raw edge and add 1". Cut 2 pieces from fabric 8" wide by the determined measurement.
12. For 1 cuff, match right sides and 8" edges and fold 1 cuff piece in half.

Using a $\frac{1}{2}$" seam allowance, sew 8" edges together. Press seam allowance open. Matching wrong sides and raw edges, fold cuff in half. Matching raw edges, insert cuff into 1 sleeve; pin in place. Using a $\frac{1}{2}$" seam allowance, sew cuff to sleeve. Fold cuff to right side of sleeve; fold cuff in half. Repeat for remaining cuff.
13. For right pocket, follow Quilt Block instructions, page 89, to make 1 quilt block. Using patterns in reverse, repeat to make 1 quilt block for left pocket.
14. (*Note:* Follow Steps 14 - 16 for each block.) For sashing, cut two $1\frac{1}{4}$" x 5" strips and two $1\frac{1}{4}$" x $6\frac{1}{2}$" strips from fabric.
15. Using a $\frac{1}{4}$" seam allowance, sew short strips to side edges of block; press seam allowances toward sashing. Sew long strips to top and bottom edges of block; press seam allowances toward sashing.
16. Matching right sides, place 1 block and 1 pocket lining fabric piece together. Using a $\frac{1}{4}$" seam allowance and leaving an opening for turning, sew pieces together. Turn right side out and press. Sew final closure by hand.
17. Pin pockets in desired positions on cardigan. Topstitch close to side and bottom edges of pockets to secure.

SKIRT

1. Wash, dry, and press skirt and fabrics.
2. Measuring $4\frac{1}{4}$" from bottom edge of skirt, measure circumference of skirt. Divide circumference by 5.25 and round up to the next whole number if necessary. The determined number is the number of quilt blocks needed for quilt block border.

3. Follow Quilt Block instructions to make the number of quilt blocks determined in Step 2.

4. (*Note:* Use a ¼″ seam allowance for Steps 4 - 9.) For sashing at sides of blocks, cut one 1¼″ x 5″ strip of fabric for each block. Sew sashing to right edge of each block; press seam allowance toward sashing. Sew blocks together into 1 row; press seam allowances toward sashing.

5. For sashing at top and bottom of row of blocks, measure 1 long edge of row. Cut 2 fabric strips 1¼″ wide by the determined measurement. Sew sashing to top and bottom edges of row of blocks; press seam allowances toward sashing.

6. Measuring 4¼″ from bottom edge of skirt, measure circumference of skirt and add ½″. Measuring from 1 end of quilt block border, trim border to the determined length. Matching right sides and short edges, fold quilt block border in half. Sew short edges together to form a loop; press seam allowance to 1 side.

7. Cut off bottom 4½″ of skirt and set aside. Cut off next 5½″ from bottom of skirt and discard.

8. With right sides facing and matching top raw edge of border to bottom raw edge of skirt, pin border to skirt. Sew border to skirt; press seam allowance toward border.

9. With right sides facing and matching raw edges, sew bottom part of skirt to bottom of border. Press seam allowance toward border.

QUILT BLOCK
Note: Refer to Diagram, page 90, to assemble block. For each sewing step, pin fabric pieces right sides together, matching sewing lines. Press seam allowances to 1 side.

1. Use felt-tip pen to trace template patterns, this page and page 90, onto acetate; cut out. Label templates.

2. (*Note:* Templates do not include seam allowances; the outline of each template pattern is the sewing line.) Leaving at least ½″ between pieces, use fabric marking pencil to draw around templates on indicated fabrics. Cut out pieces ¼″ from drawn lines.

3. Lay out all pieces except door and window appliqué pieces (templates I and J) to form block. Stitching directly on drawn lines, sew pieces into rows (Fig. 1); sew rows together.

Fig. 1

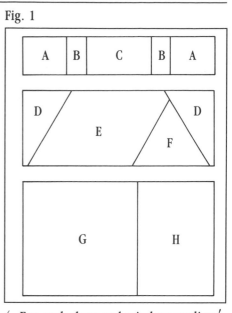

4. For each door and window appliqué, place fabric piece wrong side up on ironing board. Center template on fabric piece. Using a hot, dry iron and working on 1 small area at a time, press seam allowance over template, folding and clipping fabric as necessary so seam allowance will lie flat. After entire seam allowance has been pressed, remove template and press again.

5. Position door and window appliqués on quilt block; pin in place. Follow Hand Appliquéing, page 125, to appliqué pieces to block.

PIECING TEMPLATE A
(cut 2 from muslin)

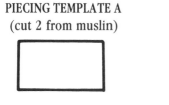

PIECING TEMPLATE B
(cut 2 from print fabric)

PIECING TEMPLATE C
(cut 1 from muslin)

APPLIQUÉ
TEMPLATE I
(cut 2 from
print fabric)

Continued on page 90

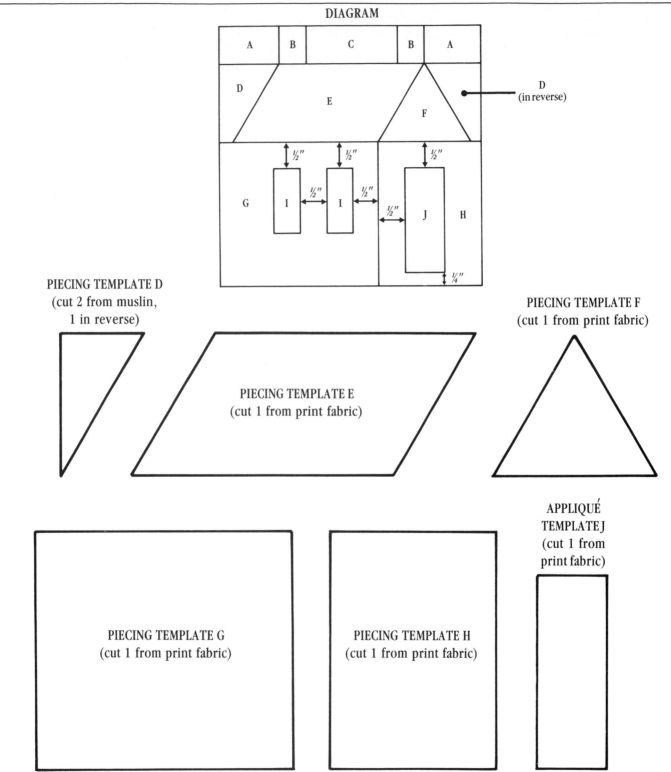

DIAGRAM

PIECING TEMPLATE D
(cut 2 from muslin,
1 in reverse)

PIECING TEMPLATE E
(cut 1 from print fabric)

PIECING TEMPLATE F
(cut 1 from print fabric)

PIECING TEMPLATE G
(cut 1 from print fabric)

PIECING TEMPLATE H
(cut 1 from print fabric)

APPLIQUÉ
TEMPLATE J
(cut 1 from
print fabric)

CLOWN COSTUME (Shown on page 66)

You will need a men's shirt, Bermuda shorts, vest, and necktie (we found ours at a thrift store); felt hat (available at craft stores); two 1½" dia. red pom-poms; yellow and green chenille stems for flower; fabric for hat band; clown shoes, wig, nose, and face paint (available at costume shops); satin ribbon for shoe laces; orange, green, purple, blue, and yellow dimensional fabric paint in squeeze bottles; 2 large buttons for sleeves; removable fabric marking pen; 18-gauge wire; seam ripper; thread to match hatband fabric, shorts, and shirt; hot glue gun; and glue sticks.

1. Referring to photo, follow Steps 3 - 6 of Dimensional Fabric Painting, page 125, to paint large dots on vest.
2. For suit, try shirt on child and use a pin to mark 1" below natural waistline. Place shirt on a flat surface and use pen to draw a line across shirt at pin mark. Cut off bottom of shirt along drawn line.
3. Button bottom of shirt. Baste ½" and ¼" from raw edge of shirt, removing button if necessary. Pull basting threads, drawing up gathers to fit waistband of shorts.
4. With waistband of shorts overlapping bottom edge of shirt 1" and matching center front of shirt to center front of shorts, place bottom edge of shirt in shorts; pin in place. Stitching close to top edge of waistband, sew shorts to shirt.

5. Measure circumference of shorts waistband; multiply by 2 and add 2". Cut a length of wire the determined measurement. Use seam ripper to make a small opening on inside of waistband. Thread wire twice through waistband; twist ends of wire together to secure.
6. Try costume on child and use a pin to mark 1" below desired length on each sleeve. Place shirt on a flat surface and use pen to draw a line across each sleeve at pin mark. Cut off bottom of each sleeve along drawn line. Press each sleeve ¼" to wrong side; press ¾" to wrong side again and stitch in place.
7. For pleats in sleeves, use pen to mark a 3½" long line 2" from top fold of sleeve. Sew along marked line (Fig. 1). Repeat for remaining sleeve.

Fig. 1

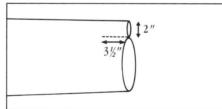

8. Referring to Fig. 2, press 1 sleeve pleat flat; sew 1 button to sleeve over pleat. Repeat for remaining sleeve.

Fig. 2

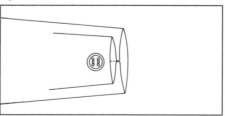

9. For tie, use dimensional paints to add desired designs to tie; allow to dry.
10. For flower on hat, cut five 6" lengths from yellow chenille stems. Form lengths into loops. Referring to photo, glue ends of loops to back of 1 pom-pom. Cut two 8" lengths from green chenille stems; twist lengths together. Glue 1 end of green chenille stem to center back of flower. Glue remaining pom-pom over back of flower. Glue stem of flower to side of hat. Allow to dry.
11. For hatband, measure circumference of hat crown; add 1". Cut a piece of fabric 4" wide by the determined measurement. Cut a 2" x 3½" strip of fabric.
12. Press long edges of large fabric strip 1" to wrong side. Press long edges of small fabric strip ½" to wrong side.
13. Overlap ends of large fabric strip 1" to form a loop; glue to secure. Wrap small fabric strip around overlapped ends. Glue to secure. Place hatband on hat.
14. Lace shoes with satin ribbon. Tie laces into bows.
15. Refer to photo to assemble costume.

You will need a sweatshirt; unbleached muslin fabric for pansies and leaves; yellow, fuchsia, violet, blue, green, and black fabric dye in squeeze bottles; thread to match fabric dyes; black permanent felt-tip pen with fine point; brown and dk brown fabric paint; large soft paintbrushes; T-shirt form or cardboard covered with waxed paper; tracing paper; item(s) to transfer patterns to fabric (see Transferring Patterns, page 124); fusible low-loft polyester bonded batting; liquid fray preventative; removable fabric marking pen; 22″ lengths of desired ribbon; and ½″ dia. VELCRO® brand hook and loop fasteners.

1. Wash, dry, and press sweatshirt and muslin according to paint and dye manufacturers' recommendations. Insert T-shirt form into shirt.
2. Use pansy, leaf, and flowerpot patterns, this page and page 93, and follow Tracing Patterns, page 124.
3. Referring to photo for placement, follow Transferring Patterns, page 124, to transfer flowerpot pattern onto shirt. Using a flat paintbrush, paint pot brown. Referring to grey areas on pattern, shade pot with dk brown; allow to dry. If necessary, heat-set flowerpot according to paint manufacturer's instructions.
4. (*Note:* Follow Steps 4 - 12 for each pansy. Practice dyeing technique on scrap fabric until desired effect is achieved.) Cut two 5″ squares from muslin. Place muslin squares on a flat protected surface. Apply an approximately 1″ diameter pool of desired color dye (except black) to center of each muslin square. Dip paintbrush in water. While dye is still wet, work wet paintbrush through dye, spreading dye over muslin.

5. For black area at center of pansy, drop 2 or 3 drops of black dye at center of 1 dyed muslin piece (front). Dip a paintbrush in water. While dye is still wet, work wet paintbrush through drops of dye, spreading dye unevenly in center of muslin square; black area should be 1″ to 1½″ wide. Allow muslin pieces to dry.
6. If necessary, heat-set dyed muslin pieces according to dye manufacturer's instructions.
7. Follow Transferring Patterns, page 124, to transfer pansy pattern to center of front muslin piece. Use black pen to draw over detail lines (indicated by dotted lines) on pattern.
8. Cut 1 piece of fusible batting slightly smaller than muslin piece. Follow manufacturer's instructions to fuse batting to wrong side of front muslin piece. Place muslin pieces wrong sides together.
9. Using a short stitch length and thread to match dye, stitch along solid and dotted lines on pansy. Cutting close to outer stitching line, cut out pansy. Apply fray preventative to raw edges of pansy.
10. For dimensional effect, fold pansy in half lengthwise with right sides together. Referring to Fig. 1 and beginning ¾″ from top of pansy, stitch a ¾″ long seam through all layers as close as possible to foldline.

Fig. 1

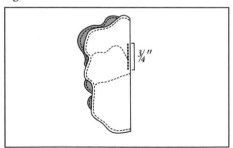

11. With right sides together, fold pansy from top to bottom along bottom black pen line. Beginning ¼″ from left side of pansy, stitch a ¾″ long seam through all layers as close as possible to foldline. Repeat for right side of pansy.
12. For yellow stitching at center of pansy, use a wide zigzag stitch with a very short stitch length to make 2 wide bar tacks (indicated by dashed lines on pattern) on pansy.
13. Using green dye and leaf pattern, repeat Steps 4 - 9 (omitting Step 5) for each leaf.
14. Tie ribbon lengths together into a bow; trim ends.
15. Arrange pansies, leaves, and bow on shirt. Use fabric marking pen to mark position of center of bow and each pansy and leaf on shirt. Sew loop side of a VELCRO® fastener at each marked dot on shirt. Sew hook sides of fasteners to back of bow and each pansy and leaf. Attach pansies, leaves, and bow to shirt.
16. Before laundering shirt, remove pansies, leaves, and bow. Follow dye manufacturer's recommendations to wash pansies and leaves. Follow paint manufacturer's recommendations to wash shirt.

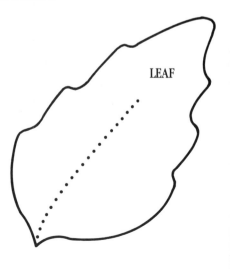

LEAF

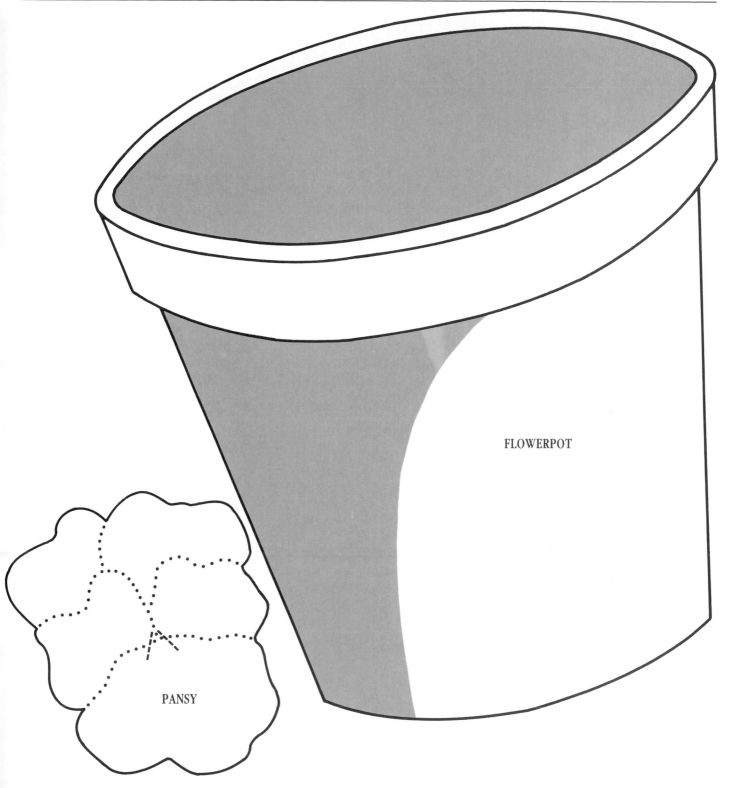

FLOWERPOT

PANSY

*W*inter

Winter's frosty weather has a special magic. The first snowfall brings out the child in everyone — who can resist the challenge of a snowball fight or building a snowman! Christmas is fast approaching, bringing fun and merriment to the season, and the anticipation of a new year is cause for celebration. For outdoor activities, we reach for our coziest casual clothes, while holiday parties call for sparkling outfits and accessories. In this collection, we offer an assortment of ideas, from casual to fancy, to help you and your family prepare for the season.

Snowman Romper, page 110

Santa's Helper Jumper, page 108

Children will love these frosty fashions! For Santa's little helper, a jumper is adorned with a three-dimensional elf appliqué and mitten-shaped pockets. A skating set for a little girl includes a skirt appliquéd with ice skates and a "fur" collar and headband made from a feather boa. To create a jolly sweatshirt, we painted it with snowflakes and a smiling snowman (he's also used to dress up the romper shown on page 95).

Skating Set, page 112
Snowman Sweatshirt, page 110

W hen the cold wind blows, you'll be warm and snug in these cozy clothes. Appliquéd penguins and snowflakes add wintry charm to a bright red sweatshirt. A pair of flannel shirts are dressed up with contrasting fabrics and a penguin pal.

Festively trimmed with Christmas motifs, men's boxer shorts make great loungewear for teens when worn over leggings or tights. Heavy socks decorated with plaid bows and appliquéd tree shapes will keep your toes nice and toasty.

Snowy Penguins Sweatshirt,
Cozy Flannel Shirt, page 123
Penguin Pocket Shirt, page 117

Festive Boxers, page 118
Toasty Socks, page 123

99

T*his country casual wear is perfect for the first days of winter! Simple shapes are appliquéd on a gold jacket and finished with blanket stitch embroidery. We used the same stitch around the edges of the coat. To create the luxuriously textured coat of many colors, a man's denim shirt is quilted with layers of fabric that are then clipped and frayed to reveal the different hues. A turtleneck is decorated with heart and star appliqués made with the same techniques.*

Heart and Stars Shirt, page 123
Blanket Stitch Blazer, page 121

Coat of Many Colors, page 119

Classic Crest Sweater, page 116

Touches of gold add elegance to these appliquéd poinsettia shirts. One features a checked ribbon and silk flowers with pearly centers. Metallic gold petals and jingle bells make the red shirt especially festive for the season.

Displayed against a checked background, a tasseled crest gives a classic look to a sweater. The crest is removable, so you can use it to dress up other garments, too.

Poinsettias and Pearls Sweatshirt, page 122
Golden Poinsettias Sweatshirt, page 111

*S*himmering metallic fabrics and paints, gold ribbon, jewels, and sequins add holiday pizzazz to the plain black turtleneck below. It's sure to appeal to teens!

Holiday Glitter Top, page 117
Ruffled Party Set, page 120

Bubble Skirt Party
Dress, page 113

Gleaming skirts transform ordinary knit shirts into dazzling party dresses for the junior high set! On the opposite page, a three-tiered ruffled skirt is teamed with a scoop-necked top and tied off with a coordinating sash; matching ruffles are slipped over the wrists for a finishing touch. The dropped-waist dress is made by adding a puffy skirt to a turtleneck. A gold rosette makes a stylish accent for the belt.

Y ou'll be the toast of any holiday gathering in this chic dress. Faux jewels and pearls adorn the neckline and pockets of a classic black dress to create this very special outfit.

Jeweled Black Dress, page 121

Elegant parties call for our finest apparel and accessories. Lace appliqués enhanced with gold beads and pearls make a stunning addition to a shimmery gold sweater. A black velvet belt and purse are treated to gold appliqués, jewels, and satin bows. The matching shoe clips can be attached to your dressiest pumps.

Beaded Appliqué Sweater, page 117
Elegant Holiday Accessories, page 122

You will need a jumper; the following fabrics for elf appliqué and pockets: 6" square of peach for face, four 4" squares of peach for ears, 7" x 10" piece of green for cap, 7" x 14" piece of white for beard, two 2" x 6" pieces of white for mustache, 9" square of white for backing, 2" x 5" piece of white felt for eyebrows, four 5" squares of blue for mitten pockets, and four 2" x 5" pieces of white for mitten pocket cuffs; thread to match fabrics; fusible low-loft polyester bonded batting; tracing paper; fabric marking pencil; 1" dia. red pom-pom; 8" of $\frac{3}{8}$"w blue satin ribbon; $\frac{3}{4}$" dia. gold jingle bell; white and black fabric paint; small round paintbrush; black permanent felt-tip pen with fine point; item(s) to transfer pattern to fabric (see Transferring Patterns, page 124); compass; washable fabric glue; cosmetic blush; and four $\frac{1}{2}$" dia. VELCRO® brand hook and loop fasteners.

1. Wash, dry, and press jumper and fabrics.
2. For face, use compass to draw a 5" dia. circle on fabric. Cut out circle.
3. Using eyes pattern, page 109, follow Tracing Patterns and Transferring Patterns, page 124, to transfer eyes to center of fabric circle.
4. Referring to photo, use black and white paint to paint eyes. Allow to dry. Use black pen to outline eyes. Apply blush below eyes.
5. Using remaining patterns, page 109, follow Tracing Patterns, page 124. Cut out patterns.
6. For beard, use pattern and cut 2 beard pieces from fabric. Place beard pieces right sides together. Using a $\frac{1}{4}$" seam allowance and stitching along inner curved edge only, sew beard pieces together. Clip curves and turn beard right side out; press.
7. For cap, use cap pattern and fabric and repeat Step 6, stitching along bottom curved edge of cap only.
8. For elf appliqué, overlap edges of beard and cap $\frac{1}{4}$". Refer to photo to glue beard, then cap, to face.
9. Following manufacturer's instructions, fuse 2 layers of batting to wrong side of elf appliqué. Trim edges even with appliqué.
10. Matching right sides, center appliqué on backing fabric. Stitching $\frac{1}{4}$" from edge of appliqué, sew appliqué to backing fabric. Trim backing fabric even with edges of appliqué. Clip seam allowance. Carefully cutting through backing fabric only, cut a 3" long slit in center back of appliqué. Turn right side out through opening. Whipstitch opening closed; press.
11. (*Note:* Refer to photo for Steps 11 - 15.) For mustache, follow manufacturer's instructions to fuse 2 layers of batting to wrong side of 1 fabric piece. Use mustache pattern and follow Sewing Shapes, page 124. Sew final closure by hand; press. Glue mustache to appliqué.
12. For each ear, use ear pattern and 1 layer of batting and repeat Step 11. Whipstitch 1 ear to each side of appliqué.
13. Use eyebrow pattern and cut 2 eyebrows from felt. Glue eyebrows to appliqué.
14. For nose, glue pom-pom to appliqué.
15. Tie ribbon into a bow. Tack bow and jingle bell to top of hat.

16. Sew hook side of fasteners to back of appliqué. Sew loop side of fasteners to jumper to match fasteners on appliqué. Attach appliqué to jumper.
17. For mitten pockets, match 1 long edge of 1 cuff piece to 1 edge of 1 mitten square with right sides together. Using a $\frac{1}{4}$" seam allowance, sew pieces together along long edge of cuff piece. Repeat for remaining mitten and cuff pieces. Press seams open.
18. Referring to Fig. 1, match dotted line on pocket pattern to seamline on 1 pocket fabric piece and follow Step 1 of Sewing Shapes, page 124.

Fig. 1

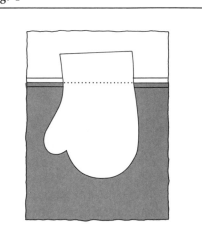

19. Matching seamlines and raw edges, place marked fabric piece and 1 unmarked fabric piece right sides together and follow Steps 2 and 3 of Sewing Shapes, page 124. Sew final closure by hand; press.
20. Repeat Steps 18 and 19 for remaining pocket.
21. Pin pockets to jumper. Stitch close to side and bottom edges of pocket to secure.
22. Remove appliqué from jumper before laundering.

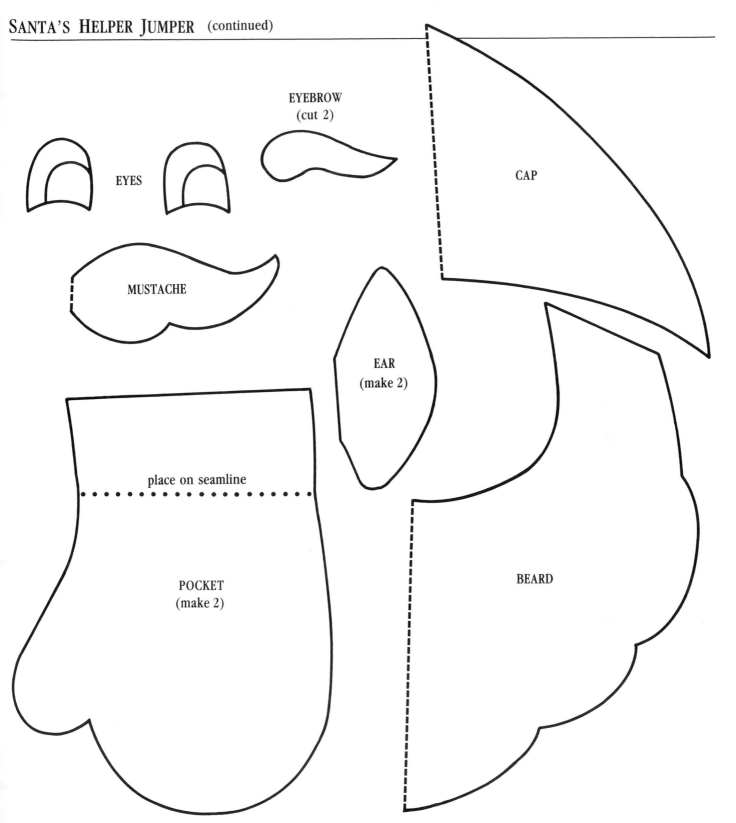

EYEBROW
(cut 2)

EYES

CAP

MUSTACHE

EAR
(make 2)

place on seamline

POCKET
(make 2)

BEARD

You will need cellulose sponges; permanent felt-tip pen with fine point; tracing paper; T-shirt form or cardboard covered with waxed paper; foam brush; white, orange, and black dimensional fabric paint in squeeze bottles; black fabric; paper-backed fusible web; lightweight fusible interfacing; see-through pressing cloth; and removable fabric marking pen.

For romper, you will also need a romper, 10″ of 1″w plaid ribbon for scarf, thread to match ribbon, washable fabric glue, and ½″ dia. and ⅜″ dia. white pom-poms.

For sweatshirt, you will also need a sweatshirt.

ROMPER

1. Use snowman and hat patterns and follow Tracing Patterns, page 124. Cut out patterns.

2. (*Note:* Refer to photo for Steps 2 - 7.) Use snowman patterns and white paint and follow Sponge Painting, page 126, to paint snowman.

3. For hat appliqué, follow Steps 2 - 5 of Making Appliqués, page 124.

4. Use fabric marking pen to draw face, buttons, and arms on snowman.

5. To appliqué hat and paint details on snowman, follow Steps 2 - 6 of Dimensional Fabric Painting, page 125.

6. For snowman scarf, fringe ribbon ends ¼″. Wrap thread tightly around center of ribbon; knot thread and trim ends close to knot. Matching ends, fold ribbon in half. Wrap thread tightly around ribbon 1¾″ from center knot; knot thread and trim ends close to knot. Position scarf on snowman and glue in place. Allow to dry.

7. For snow, glue pom-poms to romper; allow to dry.

8. To launder, follow paint and glue manufacturers' recommendations.

SWEATSHIRT

1. For snowman, follow Steps 1 - 5 of Snowman Romper.

2. For snowflakes, refer to photo and use fabric marking pen to draw snowflakes on sweatshirt.

3. To paint snowflakes, follow Steps 3 - 7 of Dimensional Fabric Painting, page 125.

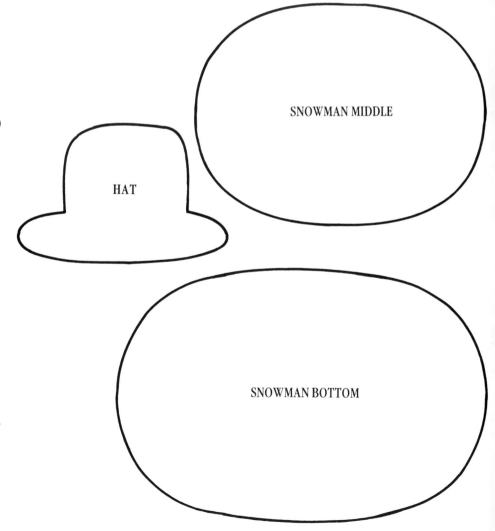

GOLDEN POINSETTIAS SWEATSHIRT (Shown on page 103)

You will need a sweatshirt; metallic gold fabric; assorted size gold jingle bells for poinsettia centers; silk poinsettia leaves; 1¼ yds of ⅞"w plaid ribbon; thread to match ribbon; gold glitter, clear, and green dimensional fabric paint in squeeze bottles; tracing paper; lightweight fusible interfacing; paper-backed fusible web; see-through pressing cloth; aluminum foil; and T-shirt form or cardboard covered with waxed paper.

1. To prepare sweatshirt, fabric, ribbon, and leaves, follow Step 1 of Poinsettias and Pearls Sweatshirt instructions, page 122.

2. For leaf appliqués, follow Steps 3 and 4 of Poinsettias and Pearls Sweatshirt instructions, page 122.

3. For petal appliqués, use petal patterns and follow Tracing Patterns, page 124; cut out patterns. Follow Steps 2 and 3 of Making Appliqués, page 124.

4. Follow Step 5 of Making Appliqués, page 124, to fuse petal and leaf appliqués to shirt.

5. Referring to photo, follow Steps 2 - 6 of Dimensional Fabric Painting, page 125, to apply gold paint to edges of petals and clear paint to edges of leaves. Use green paint to paint veins on leaves. Use gold paint to adhere several jingle bells to center of each poinsettia.

6. Tie ribbon into a bow. Cut V-shaped notches in end of each streamer. Referring to photo, arrange bow and streamers on shirt; securely tack in place.

7. To launder, follow paint manufacturer's recommendations.

DIAGRAM

PETAL A
(cut 7)

PETAL B
(cut 5)

PETAL C
(cut 5)

PETAL D
(cut 4)

■ Petal A
■ Petal B
☐ Petal C
▨ Petal D

SKIRT

You will need a skirt, one 8″ square of white fabric for boots appliqué, one 4″ x 7″ piece of silver lamé fabric for skate runner appliqués, 7″ of ⅛″w red satin ribbon, fourteen ⅛″ dia. red glass pebble beads, lightweight fusible interfacing, paper-backed fusible web, see-through pressing cloth, white and silver dimensional fabric paints in squeeze bottles, item(s) to transfer pattern to fabric (see Transferring Patterns, page 124), washable fabric glue, cardboard covered with waxed paper, and tracing paper.

1. Use boots pattern and skate runner patterns and follow Tracing Patterns, page 124. Cut out patterns.
2. (*Note:* Refer to photo for Steps 2 - 4.) Follow Making Appliqués, page 124, to make boots from white fabric and runners from silver fabric.
3. For lacings, cut fourteen ½″ lengths from ribbon. Referring to dotted lines on pattern, glue ribbons to boots.
4. To appliqué skates and paint detail lines, follow Steps 2 - 5 of Dimensional Fabric Painting, page 125. Before paint is dry, press beads into lines of paint at left of ribbon lacings. Follow Step 6 of Dimensional Fabric Painting.
5. To launder, follow paint and glue manufacturers' recommendations.

HEADBAND AND COLLAR

You will need a 1½″w tapered white headband, white marabou feather boa (available at fabric stores), two 12″ squares of white fabric, white extra-wide double-fold bias tape, white thread, 1½ yds of ¼″ dia. white velvet cording (available at fabric stores), tracing paper, compass, fabric marking pen, hot glue gun, and glue sticks.

1. For "fur" on headband, measure length of headband; cut 2 lengths from feather boa the determined measurement. Glue 1 length ½″ from each long edge of headband.
2. For collar pattern, cut a 12″ square from tracing paper; fold in half from top to bottom and again from left to right. Use compass to draw lines on paper as shown in Fig. 1. Cutting through all layers, cut out pattern along drawn lines. Unfold pattern and lay flat.

Fig. 1

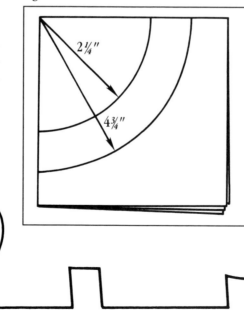

3. Referring to Fig. 2, cut front collar opening in pattern.

Fig. 2

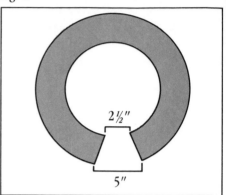

4. Use pattern and fabric squares and follow Sewing Shapes, page 124, to make collar. Sew final closure by hand; press.
5. To make cording casing, measure inner edge of collar; add 1″. Cut a length of bias tape the determined measurement. Unfold ends of bias tape and press ends ½″ to wrong side; refold tape. Insert inner edge of collar between long folded edges of binding. Sew binding to collar close to inner edge of binding. Thread cording through casing.
6. For pom-poms at ends of cording, tie a knot at each end of cording. Cut two 4″ lengths from feather boa. Wrap 1 length of feathers around each knot; glue to secure.
7. For "fur" on collar, measure outer edge of collar; cut 1 length of feather boa the determined length. Glue along collar edge. Repeat for inner edge of collar.

RUNNER

RUNNER

BUBBLE SKIRT PARTY DRESS (Shown on page 105)

You will need a knit shirt (we used a long-sleeved turtleneck), fabric for underskirt (see Step 2 for amount), fabric and net tulle for skirt (see Step 3 for amount), fabric for sash and bow (see Steps 9 and 11 for amount), one 5″ x 44″ strip of fabric for flower, 12″ of $\frac{1}{16}$″w ribbon to match sash fabric, safety pin, thread to match fabrics, and fabric marking pencil.

Note: You will need the following measurements to make this project:

Hip: measure circumference of hips 6$\frac{1}{2}$″ below waistline; add 4″ to measurement.

Length: measure from 7″ below waistline to desired finished dress length; subtract 2″.

Use a $\frac{1}{2}$″ seam allowance unless otherwise indicated.

1. Try on shirt and mark with a pin 7″ below waistline. Place shirt on a flat surface and use fabric marking pencil to draw a line across shirt at pin mark; cut off bottom of shirt along drawn line.
2. For underskirt, use hip and length measurements to cut 1 underskirt from fabric. With right sides facing and matching short edges, fold underskirt in half. Sew short edges together to form a tube; press seam open. Turn right side out.
3. For skirt, multiply hip measurement by 2. Add 6″ to length measurement. Piecing as necessary, cut 1 piece from skirt fabric and 2 pieces from tulle the determined measurements. Place skirt and tulle pieces wrong sides together; using a $\frac{1}{8}$″ seam allowance, baste pieces together. With right sides facing and matching short edges, fold skirt in half. Sew short edges together to form a loop; press seam open.

4. For bottom of skirt, baste $\frac{1}{2}$″ and $\frac{1}{4}$″ from 1 raw edge (bottom) of skirt. Pull basting threads, drawing up gathers to fit 1 edge (bottom) of underskirt.
5. Matching bottom edge of underskirt to bottom edge of skirt, place underskirt and skirt right sides together. Matching seams, adjust gathers to fit; pin in place. Sew bottom edges together; turn right side out.
6. For top of skirt, baste $\frac{1}{2}$″ and $\frac{1}{4}$″ from remaining raw edge of skirt. Pull basting threads, drawing up gathers to fit top edge of underskirt. Matching wrong sides and raw edges and matching seams, baste top edges of skirt and underskirt together.
7. Match seam of skirt to 1 side seam of shirt. Matching right sides and raw edges and easing as necessary, sew skirt to shirt. Press seam toward shirt.
8. For belt loops, cut ribbon in half. Thread a needle with 1 ribbon length; knot 1 end. At 1 shirt side seam, come up through shirt 2$\frac{1}{2}$″ above skirt seam; go down $\frac{1}{4}$″ above skirt seam. Knot remaining end of ribbon. Using remaining ribbon, repeat to make belt loop at remaining side seam.
9. For sash, add 20″ to hip measurement. Cut a strip of fabric 8″ wide by the determined measurement. Matching right sides, press strip in half lengthwise. Referring to Fig. 1, use fabric marking pencil to mark 1 end of sash as indicated by dashed line. Repeat to mark remaining end of sash. Leaving an opening for turning, sew strip together along stitching lines and long raw edge. Clip corners and trim seam allowance to $\frac{1}{4}$″. Turn right side out; press. Sew final closure by hand.

Fig. 1

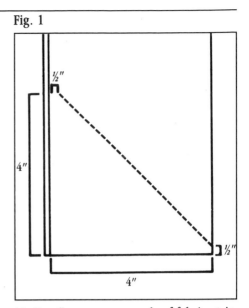

10. For flower, press ends of fabric strip $\frac{1}{2}$″ to wrong side. With wrong sides together, press strip in half lengthwise. Baste along long raw edge of strip. Pull basting thread, gathering strip to approximately 12″. Beginning with 1 short edge, loosely roll up strip. For base of flower, pinch gathered edge of strip together. Pulling stitches tight, make several stitches through pinched area to secure.
11. For bow, cut a 10″ x 18″ strip from fabric. Matching right sides, fold strip in half lengthwise. Using a $\frac{1}{2}$″ seam allowance, sew long edges together. Turn right side out. With seam at center back, press strip flat. Overlap ends of strip 2″ to form a loop; tack in place. Wrap thread several times around center of bow; knot ends of thread. Tack flower to center of bow.
12. Thread sash through belt loops and tie ends. Referring to photo, use safety pin to pin bow to sash.

SNOWY PENGUINS SWEATSHIRT (Shown on page 98)

You will need a sweatshirt; white, black, and dk yellow fabric for appliqués; black, white, orange, and dk yellow dimensional fabric paint in squeeze bottles; iridescent glitter; tracing paper; item(s) to transfer patterns to fabric (see Transferring Patterns, page 124); lightweight fusible interfacing; paper-backed fusible web; see-through pressing cloth; and T-shirt form or cardboard covered with waxed paper.

1. For penguin patterns, trace small penguin, shirt, and foot patterns and large penguin, shirt, and foot patterns, page 115, onto tracing paper. Cut out patterns.

2. For snowflake patterns, use snowflake #1, #2, and #3 patterns, this page and page 115, and follow Tracing Patterns, page 124. For snowflake #3A pattern, omit grey lines on snowflake #3 pattern, page 115, and follow Tracing Patterns. Cut out patterns.

3. Use patterns and follow Steps 1 - 4 of Making Appliqués, page 124, to make appliqués for 3 small penguins, 2 large penguins, 2 snowflake #1, 2 snowflake #2, 1 snowflake #3, and 1 snowflake #3A, transferring details to half of the penguins in reverse.

4. Follow Step 5 of Making Appliqués to fuse penguins and snowflakes to shirt. For snowflake #3A, center snowflake #3A over 1 snowflake #1 and fuse in place.

5. (*Note:* Refer to photo for Steps 5 and 6.) To appliqué penguins and paint penguin details, follow Steps 2 - 6 of Dimensional Fabric Painting, page 125.

6. To appliqué snowflakes and paint detail lines, follow Steps 3 - 5 of Dimensional Fabric Painting, page 125. While paint is still wet, sprinkle glitter over paint, coating well. Allow paint to dry. Shake off excess glitter.

7. To launder, follow paint manufacturer's recommendations.

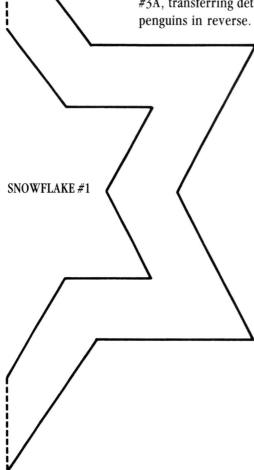

SNOWFLAKE #1

SNOWFLAKE #2

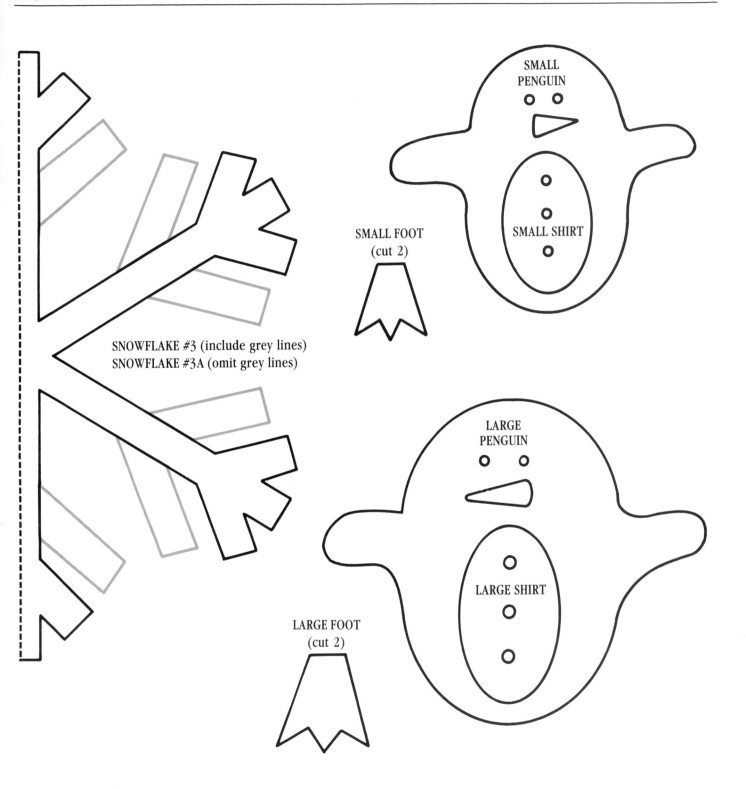

SMALL PENGUIN

SMALL SHIRT

SMALL FOOT
(cut 2)

SNOWFLAKE #3 (include grey lines)
SNOWFLAKE #3A (omit grey lines)

LARGE PENGUIN

LARGE SHIRT

LARGE FOOT
(cut 2)

Classic Crest Sweater (Shown on page 102)

You will need a sweater; one 5″ x 8″ piece of black fabric for crest; one 10″ square of fabric for background; 27½″ of ³⁄₁₆″ dia. twisted metallic gold cord; 12½″ of ⅛″ dia. metallic gold cord; 19″ of ⅛″w flat metallic gold trim; one 3″ long metallic gold tassel with hanger removed; red, green, and metallic gold acrylic paint; ½″ dia. rhinestone jewel; tracing paper; item(s) to transfer pattern to fabric (see Transferring Patterns, page 124); washable jewel glue; paintbrushes; metallic gold thread; four ½″ dia. VELCRO® brand hook and loop fasteners; see-through pressing cloth; lightweight fusible interfacing; paper-backed fusible web; medium weight fusible interfacing; and thread to match background fabric.

1. For background, use pattern and follow Tracing Patterns, page 124; cut out pattern.

2. Use background fabric and lightweight fusible interfacing and follow Steps 2 - 5 of Making Appliqués, page 124, to fuse background to sweater.

3. Stitch loop side of 1 fastener to background where indicated by each **x** on pattern.

4. Referring to photo, use metallic thread to stitch twisted metallic cord along edge of background.

5. For crest, follow manufacturer's instructions to fuse medium weight interfacing to wrong side of black fabric. Follow Tracing Patterns and Transferring Patterns, page 124, to transfer pattern to fabric.

6. Referring to photo and pattern, paint crest; allow to dry.

7. Referring to photo, glue ⅛″ dia. cord, trim, jewel, and tassel to crest. Allow to dry.

8. Trim fabric close to gold trim along outer edge of crest.

9. Glue hook side of fasteners to back of crest to match fasteners on background. Allow to dry. Attach crest to background.

10. Remove crest from sweater before laundering (crest is not washable).

X

BACKGROUND

X

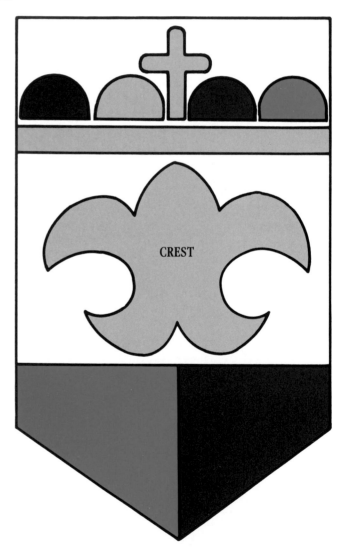

CREST

HOLIDAY GLITTER TOP

(Shown on page 104)

You will need a shirt (we used a black long-sleeved turtleneck); fabrics for appliqués; ⅜"w metallic ribbon, ¾" dia. paillettes (large round sequins with holes) and ½" dia. round jewel stones to coordinate with fabrics; gold glitter fabric paint; glitter dimensional fabric paint in squeeze bottles to coordinate with fabrics, ribbon, paillettes, and jewels; tracing paper; see-through pressing cloth; lightweight fusible interfacing; paper-backed fusible web; 1"w foam brush; chalk pencil; and T-shirt form or cardboard covered with waxed paper.

1. Wash, dry, and press shirt and fabrics according to paint manufacturers' recommendations. Insert T-shirt form into shirt.
2. (*Note:* Refer to photo for Steps 2 - 6.) Use gold fabric paint and foam brush to paint large X's on shirt; allow to dry.
3. Trace triangle pattern onto tracing paper; cut out. For triangle appliqués, use pattern and follow Steps 2 - 5 of Making Appliqués, page 124.
4. To appliqué triangles and paint wavy lines on shirt, follow Steps 2 - 6 of Dimensional Fabric Painting, page 125.
5. To adhere paillettes and jewels to shirt, follow Steps 2 and 3 of Jeweled Black Dress instructions, page 121.
6. For bows, cut ribbon into 12" lengths; tie into bows. Trim ends. Use dimensional fabric paint to adhere bows to shirt; allow to dry.
7. To launder, follow paint manufacturers' recommendations.

BEADED APPLIQUÉ SWEATER

(Shown on page 107)

You will need a sweater; large flower motifs and small flower, leaves, and stem motifs cut from gold lace; white satin for appliqué backing; 8mm ivory pearl beads; 3mm gold beads; 3mm x 6mm gold pearl beads; gold glass pebble beads; gold glass bugle beads; gold metallic thread; lightweight fusible interfacing; and liquid fray preventative.

1. (*Note*: Follow Steps 1 - 3 for each appliqué.) Cut 1 piece of satin 3" larger on all sides than 1 lace motif. Following manufacturer's instructions, fuse interfacing to wrong side of satin piece. Center lace motif right side up on right side of satin piece; pin in place.
2. Referring to photo and stitching through all layers, use a double strand of thread to sew beads to motif as follows:

    Flower and leaf outlines - bugle beads
    Centers of flowers - ivory pearl beads, 3mm gold beads, and pebble beads
    Large flower petal accents - 3mm gold beads
    Bases of leaves - pebble beads and 3mm gold beads
    Stems - 3mm x 6mm beads

3. For appliqué, trim satin close to edge of lace motif. Apply fray preventative to edges of appliqué; allow to dry.
4. Arrange appliqués on sweater. Blindstitch edges securely in place.

PENGUIN POCKET SHIRT

(Shown on page 98)

You will need a shirt with pocket large enough to accommodate large penguin design, page 115; fabric to replace pocket; thread to match fabric; white, black, and dk yellow fabrics for appliqué; lightweight fusible interfacing; paper-backed fusible web; see-through pressing cloth; item(s) to transfer patterns to fabric (see Transferring Patterns, page 124); white, dk yellow, orange, and black dimensional fabric paint in squeeze bottles; tracing paper; seam ripper; and cardboard covered with waxed paper.

1. Wash, dry, and press shirt and fabrics according to paint manufacturer's recommendations.
2. For pocket, follow Steps 7 and 8 of Cozy Flannel Shirt instructions, page 123.
3. For penguin patterns, use large penguin, shirt, and foot patterns, page 115, and follow Tracing Patterns, page 124. Cut out patterns.
4. (*Note:* Refer to photo for Steps 4 and 5.) For penguin appliqué, follow Steps 2 - 5 of Making Appliqués, page 124.
5. To appliqué penguin and paint details, follow Steps 2 - 7 of Dimensional Fabric Painting, page 125.

TRIANGLE

For each pair of boxers, you will need a pair of boxer shorts; fabrics for penguin, snowflake, or tree appliqués (we used robe velour for penguin hats and cotton fabrics for all other appliqués); lightweight fusible interfacing; paper-backed fusible web; see-through pressing cloth; tracing paper; and cardboard covered with waxed paper.

For penguin boxers, you will also need one ⅜" dia. and one ½" dia. white pom-pom; white, black, dk yellow, and orange dimensional fabric paint in squeeze bottles; item(s) to transfer patterns to fabric (see Transferring Patterns, page 124); fabric for hem trim; and thread to match boxer shorts.

For snowflake boxers, you will also need fabric for hem trim, thread to match boxer shorts, white dimensional fabric paint in squeeze bottle, and iridescent glitter.

For tree boxers, you will also need coordinating dimensional fabric paint in squeeze bottle.

PENGUIN BOXERS

1. Using small penguin, shirt, hat, and foot patterns and large penguin, shirt, hat, and foot patterns, this page and page 115, follow Tracing Patterns, page 124. Cut out patterns.
2. For penguin appliqués, use patterns and follow Making Appliqués, page 124.
3. Referring to photo, follow Steps 2 - 6 of Dimensional Fabric Painting, page 125, to appliqué penguins and paint details; do not apply paint to hats.
4. Use small dots of white paint to adhere pom-poms to points of hats. Allow to dry.
5. For hem trim, measure circumference of 1 leg opening and add 1"; cut 2 fabric strips 5" wide by the determined measurement.
6. Matching right sides and short edges, fold 1 strip in half. Use a ½" seam allowance and sew short edges of strip together to form a loop; press seam open. Matching wrong sides and raw edges, press fabric in half. With right side of trim facing wrong side of boxers, insert trim in leg opening with pressed edge of trim extending 2" beyond

bottom edge of leg. Stitch in place close to bottom edge of leg. Repeat for remaining fabric strip.
7. To launder, follow paint manufacturer's recommendations.

SNOWFLAKE BOXERS

1. Use snowflake #1 and #2 patterns, page 114, and follow Tracing Patterns, page 124. Cut out patterns.
2. For snowflake appliqués, use patterns and follow Making Appliqués, page 124. Insert cardboard covered with waxed paper into boxers.
3. Referring to photo, follow Step 5 of Snowy Penguins Sweatshirt instructions, page 114.
4. For hem trim, follow Steps 5 - 7 of Penguin Boxers instructions.

TREE BOXERS

1. Use tree and trunk patterns and follow Tracing Patterns, page 124. Cut out patterns.
2. For tree appliqués, use patterns and follow Making Appliqués, page 124.
3. To appliqué trees, follow Steps 2 - 7 of Dimensional Fabric Painting, page 125.

TREE

SMALL HAT

TRUNK

LARGE HAT

COAT OF MANY COLORS (Shown on page 101)

Note: Finished coat will be approximately 1 size smaller than original shirt. Choose shirt size accordingly.

You will need a shirt (we used a men's XL black denim shirt), 4 coordinating woven cotton fabrics for quilting (see Step 5 for amounts), fabric to match shirt for binding and plackets (see Steps 11 - 16 for amount), thread to coordinate with fabrics, small sharp scissors with fine points, seam ripper, removable fabric marking pen, and yardstick.

1. Wash, dry, and press shirt and fabrics.

2. For bottom of shirt, place shirt on a flat surface and use fabric marking pen to draw a line across bottom of shirt at desired finished length. Cut off bottom of shirt ¼" below drawn line.

3. Use seam ripper to remove pockets, collar, cuffs, plackets, and any buttons and trim from shirt.

4. Cut shirt apart by cutting off side seams, underarm seams, armhole seams, and shoulder seams. Press shirt front, shirt back (including any tucks), and sleeve pieces flat.

5. (*Note:* Follow Steps 5 - 9 for each sleeve, shirt front, and shirt back.) For quilting, cut 1 piece of each fabric approximately 1" larger on all sides than shirt piece. Layer fabric pieces wrong sides up. Center shirt piece wrong side up on fabric pieces; pin in place. Trim layered fabrics even with edge of shirt piece.

6. Using a ¼" seam allowance, stitch edges of fabrics and shirt piece together.

7. On wrong side of shirt piece, use fabric marking pen and yardstick to draw a grid of 1½" squares inside stitching lines (Fig. 1).

Fig. 1

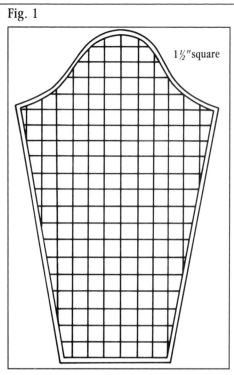

1½"square

8. Stitch along grid lines through all thicknesses of fabric.

9. Place shirt piece right side (fabric side) up. Cutting from corner to corner through top 4 fabric layers and being careful not to cut bottom layer (shirt piece), make 2 diagonal cuts across each stitched square to form an "X" (Fig. 2).

Fig. 2

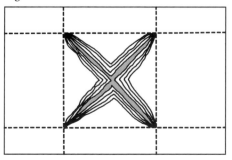

10. (*Note:* Finished seams will be on outside of coat.) Matching wrong sides and raw edges and using a ¼" seam allowance, sew shirt pieces back together in the following order: shoulder seams, armhole seams, and side seams and underarm seams.

11. To bind neckline, measure length of neckline. Cut one 1½" wide bias strip of fabric the determined measurement (pieced as necessary).

12. Press 1 long edge of strip ¼" to wrong side. With right sides facing and matching unpressed edge of binding to neckline edge, pin binding to neckline. Use a ¼" seam allowance to sew binding to coat. Press binding to wrong side of coat; whipstitch in place.

13. To bind hemline, measure around hem of coat and repeat Steps 11 and 12.

14. To bind bottom edges of sleeves, measure circumference of 1 sleeve at bottom edge; add ½". Cut two 1½" wide strips of fabric the determined measurement.

15. Match right sides and short edges and fold 1 strip in half. Using a ¼" seam allowance, sew short edges together to form a loop. Repeat for remaining strip. Repeat Step 12 for each sleeve.

16. For each front placket, measure length of coat opening; add ½". Cut 1 strip of fabric 2½" wide by the determined measurement. Press all edges of strip ¼" to wrong side. With wrong sides together, fold strip in half lengthwise; press. Insert raw edge of coat opening between folded edges of strip; baste in place. Stitch close to both long edges of placket. Spacing stitching lines ¼" apart, sew 2 lengthwise rows of stitching on placket. Remove all visible basting threads.

17. To fray raw edges of quilting, machine wash and dry coat.

Note: This garment is suitable for Junior sizes.

You will need a long-sleeved knit shirt; 2"w elastic for waistband (see Step 9 for amount); fabric for underskirt (see Step 1 for amount); coordinating fabrics for skirt ruffles, sash, and wrist ruffles (see Steps 4, 14, and 15 for amounts); tulle for underruffle (see Step 4 for amount); ¼"w elastic for wrist ruffles; 12" of ⅟₁₆"w ribbon to match sash fabric; thread to match fabrics; seam ripper; and removable fabric marking pen.

Note: Use a ½" seam allowance unless otherwise indicated.

1. For underskirt, measure hips and add 4". Measure length from waistline to 2" above knee. Cut fabric the determined measurements.

2. With right sides facing and matching short edges, fold underskirt in half. Sew short edges together to form a tube; press seam open. Press 1 raw edge (bottom) ¼" to wrong side; press ¼" to wrong side again and stitch in place. Turn right side out.

3. For placement of ruffles, refer to Fig. 1 and use fabric marking pen to mark lines around right side of underskirt.

Fig. 1

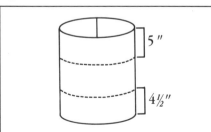

4. For ruffles, measure waistline; multiply measurement by 3. Piecing as necessary, cut three 14" wide fabric strips the determined measurement. For underruffle, cut four 5" wide strips of tulle the determined measurement; set aside.

5. Fold 1 ruffle fabric strip in half, matching right sides and short edges; sew short edges together to form a loop. Press seam open. With wrong sides together, press fabric in half lengthwise. Baste ½" and ¼" from raw edge. Pull basting threads, drawing up gathers to fit around underskirt. Repeat for remaining fabric strips.

6. For bottom ruffle, match raw edge of 1 ruffle to marked line closest to hemline; pin in place. Using a medium zigzag stitch with a medium stitch length, stitch ruffle and underskirt together ½" from raw edge of ruffle.

7. For middle ruffle, match 1 ruffle to remaining marked line and repeat Step 6.

8. For top ruffle, match raw edge of remaining ruffle to top edge of underskirt and repeat Step 6.

9. For waistband, measure waistline; add 1". Cut 2" wide elastic the determined measurement. Match right sides and short edges of elastic and sew short edges together; turn right side out. Place elastic over top of skirt, matching bottom edge of elastic to stitching line on top ruffle (elastic will cover raw edges of top of skirt). Stretch elastic to fit top edge of skirt; pin in place. Sewing through all thicknesses at bottom edge of elastic, use a medium zigzag stitch with a medium stitch length to sew elastic to skirt.

10. For underruffle, place tulle strips together and fold in half, matching short edges. Sew short edges together to form a loop; press seam open. Basting through all layers, baste ½" and ¼" from 1 raw edge. Pull basting threads, drawing up gathers to fit around underskirt.

11. To sew underruffle to underskirt, place underruffle under bottom ruffle with gathered edge of underruffle ¼" below bottom ruffle seam; pin in place. Using a medium zigzag stitch with a medium stitch length, stitch underruffle and underskirt together ½" from gathered edge of underruffle.

12. Remove all visible pen marks and basting threads; press.

13. For belt loops, cut ribbon in half. Tack ends of 1 ribbon length to top and bottom edges of elastic at each side of skirt.

14. For sash, measure waistline and add 72". Piecing as necessary, cut a 10" wide bias strip of fabric the determined measurement. Follow Step 9 of Bubble Skirt Party Dress instructions, page 113, to sew sash. Thread sash through belt loops.

15. (*Note:* For each wrist ruffle, follow Steps 15 - 18.) Measure wrist; add 1". Cut a piece of ¼" wide elastic the determined measurement. Multiply wrist measurement by 3; cut a 4½" wide strip of fabric the determined measurement.

16. With right sides facing and matching short edges, fold strip in half; sew short edges together to form a loop. Press seam open. Press 1 raw edge (bottom) ¼" to wrong side; press ¼" to wrong side again and stitch in place.

17. For elastic casing, press remaining raw edge ½" to wrong side; press ½" to wrong side again and stitch in place ⅜" from top edge.

18. Use seam ripper to open casing on wrong side of ruffle at seamline. Thread elastic through casing. Overlapping ends of elastic 1", sew ends together.

19. Referring to photo, place wrist ruffles over ends of shirt sleeves.

JEWELED BLACK DRESS

(Shown on page 106)

You will need a dress (we used a black knit dress), round and oval jewel stones in assorted sizes and colors, pearl beads, gold dimensional fabric paint in a squeeze bottle, white thread, T-shirt form or cardboard covered with waxed paper, and a chalk pencil.

1. Wash, dry, and press dress according to paint manufacturer's recommendations.
2. (*Note:* Refer to photo for Steps 2 - 4.) Arrange jewels on dress. Use chalk pencil to draw around each jewel. Remove jewels.
3. For each drawn circle or oval, refer to Steps 2 - 5 of Dimensional Fabric Painting, page 125, and fill each circle or oval with paint. Holding jewel level, press each jewel firmly into paint (paint will cover edges of jewels). Allow to dry.
4. Sew beads to dress.
5. To launder, follow paint manufacturer's recommendations.

BLANKET STITCH BLAZER (Shown on page 100)

You will need a blazer, fabrics for appliqués, coordinating embroidery floss, lightweight fusible interfacing, dry-cleanable paper-backed fusible web, see-through pressing cloth, and tracing paper.

1. Use patterns and follow Tracing Patterns, page 124. Cut out patterns.
2. For appliqués, follow Steps 2 - 5 of Making Appliqués, page 124.
3. Referring to photo, use 3 strands of floss to work Blanket Stitch (Figs. 1a and 1b) along edges of appliqués.
4. Referring to photo, use 3 strands of floss to work Blanket Stitch along edges of blazer.

BLANKET STITCH

Referring to Fig. 1a, come up at 1. Go down at 2 and come up at 3, keeping the thread below the point of the needle. Continue working in this manner, going down at even numbers and coming up at odd numbers (Fig. 1b).

Fig. 1a   Fig. 1b

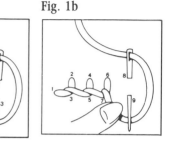

ELEGANT HOLIDAY ACCESSORIES (Shown on page 107)

BELT

You will need a belt (we used a purchased black velvet belt with black cord trim), desired metallic gold trims (we used 1″w gold appliqué trim and gold middy braid), 22″ of 1½″w satin ribbon, desired button, thread to match ribbon, and fabric glue.

1. (*Note:* Refer to photo for Steps 1 and 2.) Measure desired areas of belt for trims. Cut trims the determined measurements. Glue trims to desired areas. Allow to dry.
2. Tie ribbon into a bow. Cut V-shaped notches in ribbon ends. Securely tack button to center of bow. Glue bow to belt. Allow to dry.

EVENING BAG

You will need a handbag (we used a black velvet evening bag), 22″ of 1½″w satin ribbon, desired metallic gold trims (we used 1″w gold appliqué trim, ⅜″w gold trim, and gold middy braid), desired button, thread to match ribbon, and fabric glue.

Measure front of bag from center top to center bottom and follow Belt instructions.

SHOE CLIPS

You will need a pair of shoe clip findings, 28″ of 1½″w satin ribbon, 2 desired buttons, thread to match ribbon, and craft glue.

1. (*Note:* Refer to photo for Steps 1 - 3.) Cut ribbon in half. Tie each ribbon into a bow. Cut V-shaped notches in ribbon ends. Securely tack 1 button to center of each bow.
2. Glue 1 bow to each shoe clip. Allow to dry.
3. Attach shoe clips to shoes.

POINSETTIAS AND PEARLS SWEATSHIRT (Shown on page 103)

You will need a sweatshirt with set-in sleeves; silk poinsettia petals and leaves; 1⅔ yds of 1½″w ribbon; the following colors of dimensional fabric paint in squeeze bottles: gold glitter, red glitter, green, white pearlescent, and color to coordinate with ribbon; pearl beads and gold buttons with pearl centers (with shanks removed) for centers of poinsettias; paper-backed fusible web; see-through pressing cloth; chalk pencil; aluminum foil; safety pin; and T-shirt form or cardboard covered with waxed paper.

1. Wash, dry, and press sweatshirt and ribbon according to paint manufacturer's recommendations. Test silk petals and leaves for washability by washing 1 petal and 1 leaf. Do not use petals or leaves whose colors bleed.
2. For ribbon trim, cut two 18″ lengths of ribbon. Referring to photo, pin ribbons to shirt with 1 end of each ribbon extending beyond shoulder seam and remaining ends overlapping at center of shirt. Trim top ends of ribbons even with shoulder seams. Trim overlapped ends of ribbons to a point.
3. Remove petals and leaves from stems, discarding any plastic or metal pieces. Use a warm dry iron to press petals and leaves flat.
4. Place a large piece of aluminum foil, shiny side up, on ironing board. Place ribbons, petals, and leaves wrong side up on foil. Follow manufacturer's instructions to fuse a sheet of web to wrong sides of ribbon, petals, and leaves. Remove paper backing. Peel ribbon, petals, and leaves from foil and trim excess web.
5. Follow Step 5 of Making Appliqués, page 124, to fuse ribbons, petals, and leaves to shirt.
6. Follow Steps 2 - 6 of Dimensional Fabric Painting, page 125, to apply red paint to edges of petals, green paint to edges of leaves, and coordinating paint to edges of ribbon. Use green paint to paint veins in leaves. Use white paint to adhere pearls to centers of desired poinsettias.
7. For buttons, use gold paint and follow Steps 2 and 3 of Jeweled Black Dress instructions, page 121, to adhere buttons to centers of remaining poinsettias.
8. Tie remaining ribbon into a bow; trim ends. Use safety pin on wrong side of shirt to pin bow to shirt.
9. To launder, remove bow and follow paint manufacturer's recommendations.

TOASTY SOCKS

(Shown on page 99)

BOW SOCKS

You will need a pair of knitted slipper socks (we used socks with fake fur trim), two 2¾" x 7¾" pieces of fabric for bows, two 2½" lengths of ⅞"w satin ribbon, and thread to match fabric and ribbon.

Follow Steps 8 and 9 of School Days Denim instructions, page 76, to make 2 bows. Referring to photo for placement, tack 1 bow to each sock.

TREE SOCKS

You will need a pair of socks, fabrics for appliqués, lightweight fusible interfacing, paper-backed fusible web, coordinating dimensional fabric paint in squeeze bottle, tracing paper, cardboard covered with waxed paper, and see-through pressing cloth.

Follow Tree Boxers instructions (Festive Boxers, page 118) to apply 1 tree appliqué to each sock.

COZY FLANNEL SHIRT (Shown on page 98)

You will need a long-sleeved flannel shirt with front pocket, fabrics to cover collar and cuffs and to replace pocket, thread to match fabrics, seam ripper, paper-backed fusible web, liquid fray preventative, tracing paper, and fabric marking pencil.

1. Wash, dry, and press shirt and fabrics.
2. To cover collar with fabric, lay collar on a flat surface. Trace outline of collar onto tracing paper. Draw a line ¼" outside drawn line. Cut out pattern along outer line. Use pattern and cut 1 collar piece from fabric.
3. Clipping and folding fabric as necessary so seam allowance will lie flat, press raw edges of collar piece ¼" to wrong side.
4. Follow manufacturer's instructions to fuse web to wrong side of collar piece. Remove paper backing.

5. Matching edges, fuse collar piece to shirt collar. Stitch close to all edges of collar piece.
6. To cover cuffs with fabric, remove button from 1 cuff. Use cuff fabric and repeat Steps 2 - 5. On wrong side of cuff, cut fabric open through buttonhole. Apply fray preventative to cut edges of fabric; allow to dry. Re-sew button to cuff. Repeat for remaining cuff.
7. To replace pocket, trace pocket onto tracing paper; cut out pattern. Use seam ripper to remove pocket from shirt; discard pocket. Cut 2 pieces of pocket fabric 1" larger on all sides than pocket pattern. Use pattern and follow Sewing Shapes, page 124. Sew final closure by hand; press. Stitch across pocket through both layers 1¼" from top edge.
8. Position pocket on shirt. Sew pocket to shirt along side and bottom edges.

HEART AND STARS SHIRT (Shown on page 100)

You will need a shirt (we used a long-sleeved knit turtleneck), tracing paper, paper-backed fusible web, lightweight fusible interfacing, two 2" squares and two 4" squares of fabric for star appliqués, embroidery floss to coordinate with fabrics, five 8" squares of coordinating fabrics for heart appliqué, thread to coordinate with heart appliqué fabrics, small sharp scissors with fine point, removable fabric marking pen, see-through pressing cloth, and ruler.

1. Wash, dry, and press shirt and fabrics.

2. For each star appliqué, use star and circle patterns, page 121, and follow Steps 1 - 3 of Blanket Stitch Blazer instructions, page 121.
3. For heart appliqué, use heart pattern, this page, and follow Tracing Patterns, page 124. Cut out pattern.
4. Use pattern and cut 1 heart piece from each 8" fabric square.
5. Layer heart pieces wrong sides up; pin in place. Using a ½" seam allowance, sew pieces together.
6. Referring to Fig. 1 and marking a grid of 1" squares, follow Steps 7 - 9 of Coat of Many Colors instructions, page 119.

Fig. 1

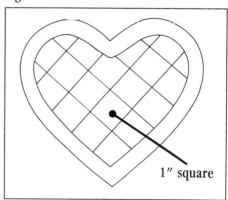

1" square

7. Clip seam allowance at ½" intervals, being careful not to clip stitching.
8. To fray edges of quilting, machine wash and dry heart appliqué.
9. Referring to photo for placement, hand stitch heart appliqué to shirt.

GENERAL INSTRUCTIONS

TRACING PATTERNS

When entire pattern is shown, place a piece of tracing paper over pattern and trace pattern, marking all placement symbols and markings.

When one-half of pattern is shown, fold tracing paper in half and place fold along dashed line of pattern. Trace pattern half, marking all placement symbols and markings; turn folded paper over and draw over all markings. Open pattern and lay flat.

TRANSFERRING PATTERNS

There are several methods for transferring patterns onto fabric. Use 1 of the following methods, depending on the weight and color of your fabric. Before transferring pattern, test chosen method on an inconspicuous area of fabric or garment.

FABRIC MARKING PEN OR PENCIL (for light-colored, lightweight or transparent fabrics) - Place pattern under fabric in desired position. Use pen or pencil to trace pattern directly onto fabric.

CHALK PENCIL (for light-colored or dark-colored fabrics) - Use dark-colored chalk pencil on light-colored fabrics; use light-colored chalk pencil on dark-colored fabrics. Use pencil to draw over lines of pattern on back of tracing paper. Position pattern, chalk side down, on garment; pin or tape to secure. Use a penny or the back of a spoon to rub over pattern. Remove pattern.

LEAD PENCIL (for light-colored fabrics) - Use soft lead pencil and follow Chalk Pencil instructions. If marks are light, they should wash out.

HOT-IRON TRANSFER PENCIL (for light-colored or dark-colored fabrics) - Use dark-colored transfer pencil for light-colored fabrics; use light-colored transfer pencil for dark-colored fabrics. Use pencil to draw over lines of pattern on back of tracing paper. Position pattern, transfer pencil side down, on fabric; pin in place. Following manufacturer's instructions, transfer design to fabric. Remove pattern.

TRANSFER PAPER (for light-colored or dark-colored fabrics) - Use dark-colored paper (sometimes called graphite transfer paper) for light-colored fabrics; use light-colored paper for dark-colored fabrics. Position pattern on garment; pin or hold in place along 1 edge. Place transfer paper, graphite or chalk side down, between pattern and fabric. Use a very dull pencil to draw over lines of pattern. Remove pattern and transfer paper.

SEWING SHAPES

1. Center pattern on wrong side of 1 fabric piece and use a fabric marking pencil or pen to draw around pattern. DO NOT CUT OUT SHAPE.
2. Place fabric pieces right sides together. Leaving an opening for turning, carefully sew pieces together directly on pencil or pen line.
3. Leaving a $\frac{1}{4}$" seam allowance, cut out shape. Clip seam allowance at curves and corners. Turn shape right side out. Use the rounded end of a small crochet hook to completely turn small areas.
4. If pattern has detail lines or markings, use fabric marking pencil or pen to lightly mark placement of lines.

MAKING APPLIQUÉS

1. For machine-appliquéd garments, wash, dry, and press garment, fabrics, and any trims. For paint-appliquéd garments, wash, dry, and press garment, fabrics, and any trims according to paint manufacturer's recommendations. Laundering instructions vary among paint manufacturers. Be sure to check labels on all brands of paints used.
2. To make appliqués, cut 1 piece of fusible interfacing and 1 piece of paper-backed fusible web slightly smaller than each appliqué fabric piece. Follow manufacturer's instructions to fuse interfacing, then web, to wrong side of each fabric piece. Do not remove paper backing.
3. Place pattern RIGHT SIDE DOWN on paper backing; use a pen to draw around pattern. Cut out each appliqué along drawn lines. Remove paper backing.
4. If pattern has detail lines or markings, place pattern right side up on right side of appliqué and follow Transferring Patterns to transfer markings to appliqué.
5. To fuse appliqués to garment, place garment face up on ironing board. Referring to project photo and/or Diagram, arrange appliqués on garment. Cover design with a see-through pressing cloth. Follow manufacturer's instructions to fuse appliqués to garment.

MACHINE APPLIQUÉING

Note: To machine appliqué, use a medium width zigzag stitch with a very short stitch length.

1. Cut a piece of rip-away backing or medium weight paper 2″ larger on all sides than design. Position backing or paper on wrong side of garment behind design; baste in place.

2. At starting point of stitching, hold upper thread forward and sew over it a few stitches. Stitch over all raw edges and detail lines of appliqué.

3. When stitching outside curves of appliqué, stop with needle positioned down on outside of curve in garment fabric and pivot or move background fabric as needed. When stitching inside curves of appliqué, stop with needle positioned down on inside of curve in appliqué fabric and pivot or move background fabric as needed.

4. When stitching outside corners of appliqué, stitch to corner and stop with needle positioned down on outside of point of appliqué in garment fabric; pivot background fabric and continue to stitch. When stitching inside corners of appliqué, stitch to corner and stop with needle positioned down on inside of point of appliqué in appliqué fabric; pivot background fabric and continue to stitch.

5. To finish, pull loose threads to wrong side of garment; knot threads and trim ends. Remove basting threads and tear away backing or paper from behind design. Remove any visible transfer marks.

HAND APPLIQUÉING

Note: Stitches in appliqué and background fabric should be equal in length and no more than ⅛″ long.

1. To appliqué shape to background fabric, bring needle up from wrong side of background fabric at 1 (Fig. 1). Insert needle in folded edge of appliqué at 2; bring needle out at 3 (Fig. 2). Insert needle into background fabric at 4; bring needle back up through background fabric at 5 (Fig. 3). Repeat until appliqué is secure.

Fig. 1

Fig. 2

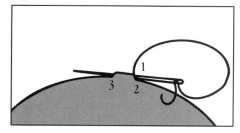

Fig. 3

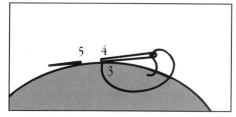

2. Knot threads on wrong side of background fabric and trim ends.

DIMENSIONAL FABRIC PAINTING

Note: Before painting on garment, practice painting technique on scrap fabric.

1. Wash, dry, and press garment and any fabrics and trims according to paint manufacturer's recommendations. Laundering instructions vary among paint manufacturers. Be sure to check labels on all brands of paints used.

2. Place garment on a flat surface. Insert T-shirt form or cardboard covered with waxed paper into garment under area to be painted.

3. Turn paint bottle upside down to fill tip of bottle before each use. While painting, clean tip often with a paper towel. If tip becomes clogged, insert a straight pin into tip opening.

4. To paint, press bottle tip against garment. Squeezing and moving bottle steadily, apply paint to garment, being careful not to flatten the paint line. If appliquéing, center line of paint over raw edge of appliqué, being sure to cover edge of appliqué completely. If painting detail lines, center line of paint over marked line on fabric.

5. To correct a mistake, use a paring knife to gently scrape excess paint from garment before it dries. Carefully remove stain with non-acetone nail polish remover. A mistake may also be camouflaged by incorporating the mistake into the design.

6. With garment lying flat, allow paint to dry following manufacturer's recommendations for drying time.

7. To launder, follow paint manufacturer's recommendations.

GENERAL INSTRUCTIONS (continued)

STENCILING

1. Wash, dry, and press garment and any fabrics and trims according to paint manufacturer's recommendations. Laundering instructions vary among paint manufacturers. Be sure to check labels on all brands of paints used.

2. For stencils, cut a piece of acetate 1″ larger on all sides than entire pattern. Center acetate over pattern and use a permanent felt-tip pen with fine point to trace the outline of all areas of 1 color. For placement guidelines, outline remaining colored areas using dashed lines. Using a new sheet of acetate for each color, repeat for remaining colored areas.

3. Place each acetate piece on cutting mat and use craft knife to cut out stencils along solid lines, making sure edges are smooth.

4. Place garment on a flat surface. Insert T-shirt form or cardboard covered with waxed paper into garment under area to be stenciled.

5. Hold or tape stencil in place. Use a clean dry brush for each color of paint. Dip brush in paint and remove excess on paper towel. Brush should be almost dry to produce a good design. Apply paint in a stamping motion. Repeat if darker color is desired. Do not use more paint on brush to achieve darker color; more paint will cause design to run or blur. Several light coats of paint will produce desired color while maintaining a clear, sharp image. Before removing stencil, allow paint to dry slightly. Remove stencil; allow to dry.

6. Matching guidelines on stencil to previously stenciled areas, repeat Step 5 for each remaining stencil.

7. If necessary, heat-set design according to paint manufacturer's recommendations.

8. To launder, follow paint manufacturer's recommendations.

SPATTER PAINTING

Note: Cover work area with paper and wear old clothes when spatter painting. Before painting garment, practice painting technique on scrap fabric.

1. Place garment on a flat surface. Insert T-shirt form or cardboard covered with waxed paper into garment under area to be painted.

2. Mix 1 part paint to 1 part water. Dip toothbrush in diluted paint and pull thumb firmly across bristles to spatter paint on garment. Repeat as desired. Allow to dry.

SPONGE PAINTING

Note: Before sponging design on garment, practice sponging design on scrap fabric.

1. Wash, dry, and press garment and any fabrics and trims according to paint manufacturer's recommendations. Laundering instructions vary among paint manufacturers. Be sure to check labels on all brands of paints used.

2. For each sponge shape, place pattern on dry sponge. To secure pattern on sponge, insert straight pins vertically through pattern and sponge. Draw around pattern using permanent felt-tip pen with fine point. Remove pattern and cut out shape.

3. Place garment on a flat surface. Insert T-shirt form or cardboard covered with waxed paper into garment under area to be painted.

4. Wet sponge and squeeze out excess water. Use a foam brush to apply paint evenly to 1 side of sponge.

5. Keeping sponge level, place sponge on garment. Lightly press down on sponge with palm of hand. Carefully lift sponge from garment. Allow paint to dry.

CROSS STITCH

COUNTED CROSS STITCH

Work 1 Cross Stitch to correspond to each colored square on the chart. For horizontal rows, work stitches in 2 journeys (Fig. 1). For vertical rows, complete each stitch as shown in Fig. 2. When the chart shows a Backstitch crossing a colored square (Fig. 3), a Cross Stitch (Fig. 1 or 2) should be worked first; then the Backstitch (Fig. 5, page 127) should be worked on top of the Cross Stitch.

Fig. 1

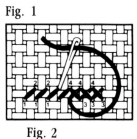

Fig. 2

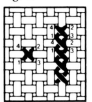

Fig. 3

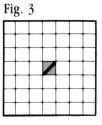

QUARTER STITCH (¼ X)

Quarter Stitches are denoted by triangular shapes of color on the chart and on the color key. Come up at 1 (Fig. 4); then split fabric thread to go down at 2.

Fig. 4

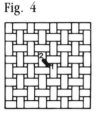

BACKSTITCH

For outline detail, Backstitch (shown on chart and color key by black or colored straight lines) should be worked after the design has been completed (Fig. 5).

Fig. 5

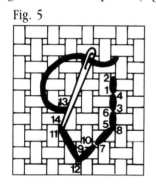

WORKING ON WASTE CANVAS

1. Cover edges of canvas with masking tape.
2. Follow project instructions to determine placement of design on garment. Mark center of design on garment with a pin. Match center of canvas to pin. Use blue threads in canvas to place canvas straight on garment; pin canvas to garment. Pin interfacing to wrong side of garment under canvas. Baste securely around edges of canvas through all 3 layers. Baste from corner to corner and from side to side.
3. (*Note:* Using a hoop is recommended when working on a large garment.) Work design on canvas, stitching from large holes to large holes.
4. Remove basting threads and trim canvas to within ¾" of design. Use a spray bottle filled with water to dampen canvas until it becomes limp. Using tweezers, pull out canvas threads 1 at a time.
5. Trim interfacing close to design.

EMBROIDERY

FRENCH KNOT

Bring needle up at 1. Wrap thread once around needle and insert needle at 2, holding end of thread with non-stitching fingers (Fig. 1). Tighten knot; then pull needle through fabric, holding thread until it must be released. For a larger knot, use more strands; wrap only once.

Fig. 1

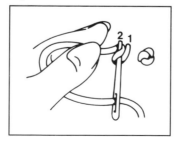

RUNNING STITCH

Make a series of straight stitches with stitch length equal to the space between stitches (Fig. 2).

Fig. 2

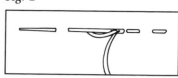

STEM STITCH

Following Fig. 3, come up at 1. Keeping the thread below the stitching line, go down at 2 and come up at 3. Go down at 4 and come up at 5.

Fig. 3

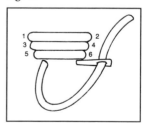

SATIN STITCH

Following Fig. 4, come up at odd numbers and go down at even numbers with the stitches touching but not overlapping.

Fig. 4

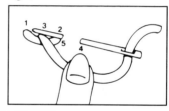

GENERAL INSTRUCTIONS (continued)

BRICK STITCH

Referring to Fig. 5, use long and short Satin Stitches, page 127, to work first row of stitching. Use long Satin Stitches to fill in remaining areas.

Fig. 5

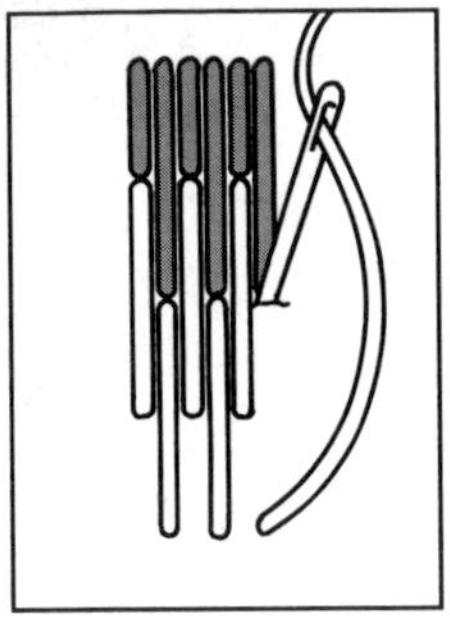

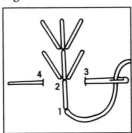

FERN STITCH

Bring needle up at 1; go down at 2 and come up at 1. Go down at 3 and come up at 4; go down at 1 (Fig. 6).

Fig. 6

LAZY DAISY STITCH

Following Fig. 7, come up at 1 and make a counterclockwise loop with the thread. Go down at 1 and come up at 2, keeping the thread below the point of the needle. Secure loop by bringing thread over loop and going down at 2.

Fig. 7

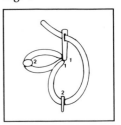

CREDITS

We want to extend a warm thank you to the generous people who allowed us to photograph our projects at their homes: Mrs. Martha Bradshaw, Mrs. Jerry Holton, Dr. and Mrs. Michael Knox, Melissa McDaniel, Nancy Newell, Gene Pfeifer, Stacy and Lee Pittman, and Mr. and Mrs. Jimmy Woodruff.

We appreciate the businesses who allowed us to photograph our projects in their facilities: Green Thumb Garden Center, Green Tree Nursery and Landscape, Holiday Inn West, Jolly Roger's Marina, Park Plaza, Pulaski Academy, and Skate City Ice and Roller Arena, all of Little Rock, Arkansas; and Crystal Hill Antique Mall of North Little Rock, Arkansas.

To Magna IV Engravers of Little Rock, Arkansas, we say thank you for the superb color reproduction and excellent pre-press preparation.

We especially want to thank photographers Ken West, Larry Pennington, and Mark Mathews of Peerless Photography and Jerry R. Davis of Jerry Davis Photography, all of Little Rock, Arkansas, for their time, patience, and excellent work.

To the talented designers who helped in the creation of many projects in this book, we extend a special word of thanks.

Ladies' Monogram, page 26, and *Baby T-Shirts*, page 35: Lorraine Birmingham
Sunflower Shirt, page 51, and *Mermaid Cover-up*, page 57: Linda Lovette

Dad's Hats, page 58: Sam Hawkins
Autumn Leaves Sweater, page 79: Kathy R. Bradley
Little Jack-O'-Lantern Shirt, page 83: Lecia P. Bain

We extend a sincere thank you to all the people who assisted in making and testing the projects in this book: Kim Camp, Mary Carlton, Trudi Drinkwater, Helen Hood, Cindy Miller, Patricia O'Neil, Sandy Pigue, Lavonne Sims, Karen Sisco, Lea Ann Smith, Helen Stanton, Amy Taylor, Karen Tyler, and Sharon Walker. A special word of thanks is given for the busy hands of Jennie Black, Kelly Hepner, and Kathy Jones.